"What I love about this book is that it is not just a theory or a short-term fix for uplifting emotional feelings to try and gain hope. Mark writes from real gut-wrenching stories, not just happy or cliche ones, and does not avoid the reality of struggling to gain hope or admitting it is often difficult even as a Christian. It brings me joy thinking of all those who will read this and how uplifted they will be when they understand that real hope is possible."

**Dan Kimball,** pastor, Vintage Faith Church, author, *They Like Jesus but Not the Church*

"I'm a fan of happiness, and looking for the silver lining seems healthy. But I don't think most people—myself included—find 'be happy' or 'look for the positive' admonitions to be all that helpful when struggling with pain, sorrow, injustice or stuckness. Oestreicher redefines hope, or better yet, pulls us back to a workable set of postures for receiving hope. This book reminds us that hope is a beautiful gift, an influx of Jesus into our dark and dry souls."

**David Crowder,** recording artist

"Using profound illustrations, engaging personal stories and a deep biblical framework, Oestreicher takes us on an exciting journey—a journey to rediscover hope and the life that it brings. *Hopecasting*'s thesis is simple, but the implications for our lives are profound. Read this book; your life may never be the same again."

**Jim Belcher,** president, Providence Christian College

"Having spent thirty-plus years working and speaking in churches, I am so excited for *Hopecasting* to find its way into sermons and congregations—an important message that will make all the difference in the vitality of the local church. I would love to see church leaders use this wonderful book to stir up conversations, prayer and action toward becoming beacons of 'hopecasting' in their communities. I'm grateful for Mark's challenge to see and live life differently."

**Doug Fields,** teaching pastor at Saddleback and Mariners Church

"Mark Oestreicher offers deep encouragement for those of us who have ever struggled to cultivate transformative hope in hard places. Drawing on personal experience, he offers a practical path for pushing through fear and cynicism, toward refreshing hope. I am grateful for the invitation Mark offers us here—an invitation into active, faithful confidence in the goodness of God."

**Gary A. Haugen,** president and CEO, International Justice Mission

# HOPECASTING

Finding, Keeping and Sharing the Things Unseen

*Mark Oestreicher*

IVP Books

An imprint of InterVarsity Press
Downers Grove, Illinois

InterVarsity Press
P.O. Box 1400, Downers Grove, IL 60515-1426
ivpress.com
email@ivpress.com

InterVarsity Press® is the book-publishing division of InterVarsity Christian Fellowship/USA®, a movement
of students and faculty active on campus at hundreds of universities, colleges and schools of nursing in the
United States of America, and a member movement of the International Fellowship of Evangelical Students.
For information about local and regional activities, visit intervarsity.org.

All Scripture quotations, unless otherwise indicated, are taken from THE HOLY BIBLE, NEW
INTERNATIONAL VERSION®, NIV® Copyright © 1973, 1978, 1984, 2011 by Biblica, Inc.™ Used by
permission. All rights reserved worldwide.

While any stories in this book are true, some names and identifying information may have been changed to
protect the privacy of individuals.

Cover design: Cindy Kiple
Interior design: Beth McGill
Images: William Huber/Stone/Getty Images

ISBN 978-0-8308-3692-5 (print)
ISBN 978-0-8308-9758-2 (digital)

Printed in the United States of America ∞

green
press
INITIATIVE
As a member of the Green Press Initiative, InterVarsity Press is committed to protecting the
environment and to the responsible use of natural resources. To learn more, visit
greenpressinitiative.org.

**Library of Congress Cataloging-in-Publication Data**
Oestreicher, Mark.
  Hopecasting : finding, keeping and sharing the things unseen / Mark
Oestreicher.
    pages cm
  Includes bibliographical references.
  ISBN 978-0-8308-3692-5 (pbk. : alk. paper)
  1. Hope—Religious aspects—Christianity. I. Title.
  BV4638.O36 2015
  234'.25—dc23
                                                                    2015000960

P   21   20   19   18   17   16   15   14   13   12   11   10   9   8   7   6   5   4   3   2   1
Y   33   32   31   30   29   28   27   26   25   24   23   22   21   20   19   18   17   16   15

For those struggling to find Hope

*We also glory in our sufferings, because we know that suffering produces perseverance; perseverance, character; and character, hope. And hope does not put us to shame, because God's love has been poured out into our hearts through the Holy Spirit, who has been given to us.*

ROMANS 5:3-5

*Now faith is confidence in what we hope for and assurance about what we do not see.*

HEBREWS 11:1

*Hope, on one hand, is an absurdity too embarrassing to speak about, for it flies in the face of all those claims we have been told are facts. Hope is the refusal to accept the reading of reality which is the majority opinion; and one does that only at great political and existential risk. On the other hand, hope is subversive, for it limits the grandiose pretension of the present, daring to announce that the present to which we have all made commitments is now called into question.*

WALTER BRUEGGEMANN, *THE PROPHETIC IMAGINATION*

# CONTENTS

# FOREWORD

Imagine you are one of the twelve disciples, which for all of us is a bit of a stretch and if it isn't . . . well, let's move on. Imagine now that you are in Jerusalem that last week, that you have Passover with Jesus (before everyone doctored it into words like "communion" and "mass"). Imagine you see the guards come in the garden, and that you watch (near Peter, in fact) what they are doing to Jesus. You then stand well out of sight when Jesus is crucified, thinking about all you had hoped for, all you had planned, and all you had dreamed—and dreamed and dreamed—about the kingdom Jesus so often announced and illustrated and embodied.

Boom. In one day it is all over. Your hopes are wrecked and you wonder what to do with your life. You sense the desert and exile. Can you return to Galilee and fish? How could you ever go to synagogue again and listen to the rabbis after you had walked with Jesus and heard such brilliance and insight and spiritual reformation? Standing there in Jerusalem you may well decide to chuck it all. If they did that to Jesus, what difference does it make?

Now imagine that after Sunday morning you heard this impossible story that Jesus was not in the tomb, that a few women and other disciples had actually encountered Jesus.

And then, when no one is looking, you wander over to the tomb of Jesus, and look inside and then enter. He really is gone. You stand there and a fresh wind of something altogether new fills the tomb, and your eyes fill with tears, and you begin to recall those miracles of Jesus, the bread and the baskets, and the time he told the waves to knock it off and they listened! You start to remember all his teachings, those astounding lessons on the hills around Capernaum, all his parables, and you take a seat in the tomb and the wind gets stronger.

You begin to hope. No . . . you *hope*.

Now you are standing in the empty tomb facing the city, looking over the city up to Galilee, and the wind suddenly gets stronger—you want the world to hear about Jesus. Standing there in the empty tomb looking out you suddenly realize the world and history have changed. God has done something never done before: he has sent his Son into the enemy camp. The enemy exiled the Son but the Son reversed the exile. Jesus crossed the river of death in the resurrection, and new creation entered into history.

Hope becomes your innermost infection. Hope becomes the way to live, not just hope for the afterlife but hope in the here and now because the stone was rolled away in front of that tomb and you've tasted that empty tomb.

Reading this wonderfully encouraging, biblically shaped but genuinely honest reflection on Marko's own exile and rediscovery of a deeper hope led me to the above reflections and to Eugene Peterson's (America's pastor of pastors) golden expression: "practicing resurrection." *Hopecasting* takes us through the joy of holy week, into the exile of darkness and hopelessness, and into the empty tomb of hope. In this book Marko teaches each of us how he has learned to practice a life of hope through the resurrection.

What a gift of God this book is. May you discover the reality of a biblical hope that reshapes life today.

*Scot McKnight*
*Professor of New Testament*
*Northern Seminary*

# ON THE SERVICE ROAD

I was chatting with my friend Alex while noshing on what is quite possibly the world's best barbecue-glazed pork belly, served at a funky walk-up restaurant in San Diego called Carnitas' Snack Shack. At thirty-three years old, Alex has already had a couple career paths and multiple holding periods requiring far-less-than-satisfying work in retail.

Alex's journey has included significant chapters involving identity, others focused on vocation, and plenty of ups and downs in both family and other relationships. Alex loves Jesus and has never really faltered much in his faith. Extremely knowledgeable and gifted in music, production, preaching, interpersonal skills and a variety of other areas, Alex isn't the only one who would have predicted big success in his life (I remember meeting him a decade ago and thinking: *This guy is going to succeed at whatever he does!*). I even hired him. Twice!

But over and over again, Alex has felt stuck, unable to get from *here* to *there*. Hopeless.

I've always appreciated Alex's willingness to be both honest and articulate, so I asked him—fairly bluntly—to describe his thoughts and feelings. He told me about how some life losses had led to periods of significant depression. He told me, "When there was a logic to whatever roadblock was in my way, it was bearable, even if I didn't agree with the logic. But things were really hard when there didn't seem to be any logic."

Alex used an illustration of the thinking many of us—myself included—have toward exercise: if I exercised I'd have more energy, but I don't have the energy to exercise. He then continued, "If I could figure out what my next step is, that might give me the energy to move forward. But I don't have the energy to take the next step."

Alex was very transparent about his feelings: "There's a frustration with myself. I'm thirty-three years old, and have always been an overachiever. I should be able to figure this out. I feel like I'm letting myself down and letting other people down, even though they're not imposing expectations on me."

I had finished my plate of pork belly, and Alex had hardly been able to start his. But I wasn't about to interrupt him because he was putting such universal and resonant words to the experience of so many. I was thinking about asking how this two-steps-forward-two-steps-back existence—this hopelessness—was expressed in his prayers. But he beat me to it, saying, "I pray, 'God, why would you give me these obvious passions and talents and gifts and then have me in a place where I'm not able to use them?'"

Ouch. Alex was naming the gap between his experience and the life he dreamed of. Other versions of that gap might look like this:

*I want more than anything to live a passionate life; but I can't seem to find anything that I can connect my passion to.*

*I don't care much about material things, but I want a life of meaning. I just have no idea how to get from my current life to a life of meaning when I have to constantly give all my energy and attention to surviving day to day.*

*I have a job, but I want to do something more significant. The problem is, I don't have a clue what that would be.*

*I thought I was on the right track, but I can't seem to unlock the combination to lasting relationships where I can experience the sort of unconditional love I long for.*

*I wish I were more confident about my faith, and wasn't constantly in a seasonal cycle of doubt and disbelief.*

*I long for this pain to stop. It saps my energy and focus and leaves me perpetually ornery.*

*I am just sick and tired of not having enough money to make ends meet. It feels like I'm in a perpetual dead end and will never, ever get out of this financial hole.*

Alex expressed the gap in vivid imagery: "I feel like I'm on the access road, the service road, but I want to be in the carpool lane to the hopeful life I envision, and I can't seem to find the on-ramp. I want to grasp and control the things from the past that looked like they were taking me in the right direction, but I also know that those are in the past, and they won't ultimately take me there. I need a new vehicle."

Wow. Maybe you read that and thought, "Yup, I think I might need a new vehicle too."

ONE

# I WANT HOPE

I'm a Hope junkie, impossibly caught in its grasp. But it's a fairly new fixation for me, stemming from the trajectory change I experienced in my understanding of Hope a few years ago.

In early February of 2010, less than one month after the devastating earthquake that nearly destroyed the small half-island country of Haiti, I crossed the border from the Dominican Republic in a tiny van with eight youth workers. We were on a fact-finding trip. We knew church groups would be thinking of sending groups to help, but the constant message in the news those days was, "Don't come unless you are trained medical personnel or in construction; you'll just be in the way."

"Stay away" isn't a pill easily swallowed, and this team of youth workers I had organized were chosen for their ability to massively leverage the Internet to speak to our peers (by the way: we found that there were more than enough opportunities to help for *anyone* willing to help).

Crossing the border that day, I was nervous. I knew I was going to come face-to-face with pain and suffering to a degree I had never experienced.

What I wasn't expecting—what completely caught me off guard—was Hope.

The suffering was omnipresent. Every single person we met had lost a loved one, a home or both. Mounds of rocks in the streets covered bodies that had not yet been removed. All services, from banking to trash removal to shopping to water supplies, were shut down. Thousands of people were gathering in impromptu shantytowns, living in handmade tents pieced together with sheets and cardboard over frames made of sticks. Even those whose homes had not been lost were sleeping in similar tents, outside their cracked and unstable houses, completely terrified to once again sleep in a space that had killed so many others.

## ROODY'S REDEMPTION SONG

Just prior to crossing the border from the Dominican Republic into Haiti, we stopped at a collection of large tents—a field hospital—run by the United Nations. Dozens of patients with a wide variety of ailments and needs lay on cots, with European doctors and nurses making rounds. When a nurse heard our response to the question of why we were there, she said, "Oh, you need to talk to Roody!"

Roody was a twenty-something young man with a crushed leg immobilized in a contraption that looked like it was made of metal Tinkertoys driven into his leg at various points. He told us that his parents and sisters had died in the earthquake. His home had been destroyed. His workplace was gone.

But Roody was smiling—a beautiful toothy grin that flowed naturally as if it were connected by levers to a gut-level sense of something good. One of our team members made me uncomfortable when he asked if Roody would pray for him. I had been selfishly and myopically thinking that *we* should pray for *him*, not the other way around. But pray Roody did, beautifully and effortlessly.

The nurse had mentioned that Roody—who spoke English, and told us he'd learned it by watching American music videos—had a beautiful singing voice.

We asked Roody if he would sing for us. And right there in the blustery hot tent, laying flat on a cot, Roody shyly but clearly sang out Bob Marley's "Redemption Song."

Roody grinned as he sang, but the complexity of his angelic face and the lyrics and the brutal context of his experience stirred a profound *something* in my soul. Roody possessed something that lifted him out of his experience. Heaven coming to earth.

## MICHELLE'S SUFFERING

Our first stop across the border, just a few minutes after leaving Roody, was a tiny remote hospital on the grounds of a church. The pastor was also a doctor and found his hospital filled with patients in the days following the earthquake, even though it was more than an hour from the worst chaos. But by the time we visited, there was one remaining patient, a woman named Michelle. She wore a complicated metal brace on her grotesquely swollen right leg, almost exactly like the contraption on Roody's leg. We learned her leg had been pulverized when her home collapsed on top of her.

Through the doctor, who acted as our interpreter, Michelle soberly shared her story:

I was in my home with my twin fifteen-month old sons when the earthquake hit. As the house started to shake violently, I quickly grabbed my sons, one in each arm. The two-story concrete house fell on top of us, burying us deep under a large pile of rubble.

One of my sons was killed instantly when the house fell. I felt wetness on me, and realized it was his blood. I stretched my neck to find a way to look down where he was, and saw that he was in pieces. I had to push the pieces away from me.

My other son was alive, but barely. I could tell that his breathing was shallow, and that he had been badly wounded. I held him close to me, occasionally trying to yell for help. After waiting for a few hours, my second son died in my arms. With the concrete pinning me down and surrounding me on that side of my body, I held my son as he grew cold and lifeless. And I waited . . . for three days.

I was later told that my husband had run home from work after the earthquake. Seeing the pile of cement that used to be our house, he assumed we were all dead, and went temporarily insane. He wandered the streets for days, and has no memory of this time.

On the third day, I heard a man yelling at my pile of concrete, asking if anyone was alive. Having no food or water for three days, I was very weak, but managed to call back to him.

Now it's unclear whether or not my leg will be saved.

She registered no emotion while telling us this story. But each of us had tears streaming down our faces. We offered the only thing we could: our prayers. And as we gathered around Michelle, she asked if her husband could join us. It was only then that we realized a man sitting in the back of the room was the man who had gone temporarily insane, wandering the streets of Port-au-Prince, assuming his entire family had been instantly killed.

Michelle's husband joined her, sitting on the edge of her bed as we began to pray. During our time of prayer, Michelle sat quietly, hands open to heaven, somberly waiting to receive something, anything. But in the middle of our prayer, her husband began to cry out.

It started as a whisper in Creole: *Why, Jesus?* As he repeated the phrase over and over and over again, the volume grew until it was a full-throated wail, a desperate pleading, begging Jesus for a sliver of understanding, a shred of explanation.

## WHAT ROODY HAD

Both Roody and Michelle had experienced deep, potentially crippling trauma. Both had experienced significant physical injury, and profound personal loss. One might suggest that Michelle's ordeal was an even greater tragedy than Roody's; but only incrementally, as if Michelle scored a 99 on some 100-point pain index, and Roody merely scored 96.

Maybe Roody was an incurable optimist? While that's probably the most common explanation, the easiest answer and the one our culture would lead us to conclude, I shudder to even write that possibility in proximity to Michelle's story. Concluding that Roody's outlook is simply a result of his optimism necessitates that we label Michelle a pessimist. And I'd like to believe that none of us are willing to apply that label on her.

Even softening Michelle's outlook to that of a realist leaves us in an uncomfortable, and seemingly inaccurate place. If anything, Michelle's experience would be better labeled as *surrealism*.

Each of these labels dehumanizes Michelle and her story. That's why we are rightly uncomfortable with the labels.

Here's the catch, though: labeling Roody's outlook as optimism equally dehumanizes him, implying that he either chose to ignore his pain, or was willing to paste a smile on his face and sing about redemption. That sort of surface-y conclusion simply doesn't do justice to *his* pain. Citing optimism as Roody's source of strength minimizes his story, dismisses his dead family, diminishes the truth.

No, Roody wasn't merely an optimist. Roody had Hope, somehow, against all odds. Roody was able to hold on to something outside (above? beyond?) his current, very present reality. And while we might wrongly believe that Hope and optimism are synonymous, Roody intrinsically knew the difference.

## TOWARD DEFINING HOPE

If deep, meaningful, life-giving Hope isn't merely optimism or wishful thinking, then what is it?

Since we use *hope* in so many ways, the dictionary rightly offers multiple definitions. Two are particularly helpful here.

Let's call the first one definition A:

*To want something to happen or be true.*

And the second one, definition B:

*Kenya*
*Ghana*

*To cherish a desire with anticipation.*[1]

Definition A is a way of describing wishful thinking:

*I hope they serve pizza at lunch today.*

*I hope I get this job.*

Or even wishes that are less about me:

*I hope the damage from that storm doesn't result in a loss of life.*

*I hope my coworker experiences some joy in her life today.*

There's nothing wrong with optimism or wishful thinking (assuming what's wished for isn't evil). I am strongly in favor of wishful thinking. And looking back over those four examples above, I am unashamed to state that I have wished for every one of those, some many times.

Wishful thinking, though, has two *potential* problems embedded in it. First, wishful thinking is too easy to confuse with the sort of Hope we're focusing on in this book. I'd rather we didn't use the same word for both variations—it would make things clearer and more helpful.

The second potential problem with the wishful thinking version of hope (which some might call "positive thinking") is that it doesn't actually change anything. It's passive. The problem isn't in a wish's inability to change, but in our delusion that it can (or does).

Dave Eggers's novel *The Circle* has a hyperbolic (but too close to home) example of the impotence of wishful thinking. The story is set in the near future, in the context of a global social media company that is fairly quickly changing every form of human interaction. There are clear assumptions being made by the company (and the narrator) that are obviously flawed to us as readers. At one point, the narrator is talking about the activities of her day, and mentions in

passing her plans to attend a "fundraiser" for a school in rural Pakistan.
Later, she reports:

> The Pakistan fundraiser was thoroughly inspiring—the event
> was able to amass 2.3 million smiles for the school.[2]

Learning about the needs of a rural school in Pakistan is a good thing.
I would want that for anyone. And clicking a "smile" button (the
novel's implied equivalent to a Facebook "like") is good in a sense. But
we all know the school needs more than well-wishes, even if the well-
wishing is multiplied 2.3 million times. For anything to change at that
school, they'll need money, or sweat, or guidance, or any number of
other responses that all fall under the banner of *action*.

This calls to mind James 2:15-16:

> Suppose a brother or a sister is without clothes and daily food. If
> one of you says to them, "Go in peace; keep warm and well fed,"
> but does nothing about their physical needs, what good is it?

Back to the dictionary's definition B of hope: *To cherish a desire with
anticipation.* While this definition isn't perfect (and doesn't reveal all
the spiritual dimensions I long for you to see), it's a really wonderful
starting point.

If it were only about the desire, it wouldn't be much different than
the other definition. Desire, it should be stated, is a good thing. A gift
from God. Sure, desire can be distorted and debased, much like most
things, but the Bible is clear that God *desires* to give us the *desires* of
our hearts (Psalm 37:4).

But there are two wonderful modifications that give a substantive
recalibration to dictionary definition B.

*Anticipation* is such a great word. I get all wiggly and happy just
typing it. It's a word pregnant with all sorts of other powerful implications: confidence, receiving a gift, expectancy, probability.

Sure, one can anticipate a blow to the head, and that's certainly not a happy thought, but in general *anticipation* is a word we associate with good things definitely coming.

And when we connect it with the other modifying word in the definition—*cherish*—the whole thing starts to sound like Christmas morning.

People buy glasses or goggles with various colored lenses in order to help them see certain things. Yellow or orange lenses filter light to heighten contrast in overcast or low-light conditions. Amber or red lenses heighten contrast in partly cloudy or sunny conditions. Copper and brown lenses block high amounts of light to help vision against a backdrop of grass or blue skies. Green lenses only slightly increase contrast, while keeping color balance otherwise preserved. And gray lenses are good for normal color recognition in bright light.

I like to think of my Christian worldview as colored lenses: Jesus goggles.

Webster's dictionary isn't attempting to present a Christian worldview, of course. But when I consider definition B—*to cherish a desire with anticipation*—through my Jesus goggles, I think we're getting closer to a sound, biblical definition of Hope. *To cherish* (with God) *a desire* (because God wants to give us the desires of our hearts) *with anticipation* (of God's rescue, and of partnering with God in bringing goodness).

## HOPE IN ACTION

Hope isn't something we can drum up within ourselves. Hope is a gift, given to us when Jesus draws near to us in the time of our honesty and fear.

But Hope immediately takes us to action (another difference between biblical Hope and wishful thinking). Hope brings with it, inseparably, an invitation to partner with God; we bring our actions into *alignment* with God's actions, in *response* to God's actions. Prior to Hope's arrival, we don't have a clear sense of what, exactly, a new reality might hold. At best, our perspective is somewhat limited to "not my current experience."

Hope arrives and whispers: step into *this* new reality, *this* new possibility, *this* vision. And we are drawn to action.

I may be completely lacking in power to change my reality; but I'm invited to partner with a God—*the* God—who has more than enough power. And (this is a BIG deal), God seems to want to partner with us. Throughout the Bible and throughout all recorded history and in the lives of our friends and modern-day saints, we see God partnering with humans to bring redemption and healing.

This partnering offer is not to say that God couldn't do it without us. Instead, it seems to be a loving God's way of sharing.

My friend, author and pastor Bryan Loritts, shared a wonderful metaphor for this at an event I'd invited him to speak at recently. I resonated with the example because I am on airplanes way too much and care way too much about my frequent flier status.

Bryan shared how his frequent flying has given him a certain "status" with his airline. And that status sometimes results in free upgrades to first class. Taking the first-class seat is a no-brainer, except when he's flying with his wife, who has no status with the airline. He said he'd learned the hard way that sitting in first class while his wife sits in coach does not strengthen his marriage.

So his practice, on those occasions, is to take the seat next to his wife. And when the person whose seat he's in shows up, usually a bit miffed at his imposition, Bryan hands them his first-class seat and the showdown is immediately over.

Bryan made this connection: in giving up the better seat, "I haven't lost my status; I just refused to use my status for my own benefit."[3]

That's what God does when inviting us to partner in a life of Hope. God's not becoming less God by inviting us into co-creating; instead, God is revealing parental love. Like a human father who invites his young son to join him in swinging a hammer during a home repair project, we get included because of love, and God *enjoys* our coworking.

With all of that in mind, here's my definition of Hope:

> *Hope is faithful confidence that God continues to author a story that moves us from vision to action.*[4]

## CAUGHT OFF-GUARD BY HOPE

After our Haiti team left Michelle, we worked our way into the city and discovered the scenes we had all viewed on TV and in magazines playing out in three dimensions before our eyes. Leveled buildings, piles of rubble hiding bodies, complete chaos.

At one point, traffic came to a standstill. Straining to see what was causing our delay, we noticed that a cross street ahead was closed down, and that hundreds of people were standing in the street. We assumed it was a demonstration of some sort, people demanding help, begging for justice in a crisis where massive quantities of aid coming in by the ship-full were not actually reaching those who needed it most.

Being an adventurous lot (and feeling claustrophobic in our cramped little van), our group piled out to explore. As we approached the cross street, we saw a thousand people moving about, singing in Creole. My initial assumption was that they were singing some sort of protest song.

But as I stood on the edge of the street, I noticed a few things in rapid succession. There was a stage at the far end of the street with a band playing. The band looked suspiciously like a worship band. The people in the street were smiling, and both singing and dancing with abandon. Then it struck me: these people are worshiping, praising God!

I had a sudden urge to feel something, to explore the disequilibration in my brain and compulsion in my stomach. I separated from my group and pushed my way deep into the crowd. Two old women grabbed my hands and demanded, with their eyes, that I join in the dance (lame, fat, white-boy dancing, if I'm honest).

I remember my thoughts from that moment as clearly as if I were thinking them for the first time as I write this: *These people have all experienced a level of pain and suffering more profound than I will likely ever experience in my lifetime. And yet, here they are, singing praises to Jesus, overflowing with Hope.*

Even though I memorized a good bit of Scripture as a child, thanks to my family's participation in a recite-verses-for-neat-prizes program called the Bible Memory Association, I haven't often had verses pop into my head at opportune moments. But in that moment of confusion, a Bible passage I'd memorized as a child immediately scrolled across my brain:

> We also glory in our sufferings, because we know that suffering produces perseverance; perseverance, character; and character, hope. And hope does not put us to shame, because God's love has been poured out into our hearts through the Holy Spirit, who has been given to us. (Romans 5:3-5)

My next thought, still jumping around awkwardly in a hand-holding dance with two elderly Haitian women amidst a crowd of a thousand worshipers was, for me, revolutionary: *These people know Hope in a way I never will, because of their suffering.*

The bolts on my misguided and untested assumptions about Hope rattled hard, and suddenly broke free. I wept openly, still jumping up and down in the middle of the street. I longed for a deeper experience of Hope. I saw how tame and civilized and simplistic and affluent-American my understanding of hope was—and how unhelpful.

## THE BIG AH-HA

Standing in that crowded Haitian street, surrounded by Hope-filled worshipers who were still in the midst of almost overwhelming suffering, an ah-ha came to me. It rocked me because it concurrently smacked of the kingdom of God *and* seemed so deeply counterintuitive.

The journey to Hope—real Hope, deep Hope, Hope that stretches well beyond optimism and wishful thinking—often leads us through terrain we'd rather avoid. Hope is a gift, not the result of effort. But there are some essential actions we can take to prepare ourselves. Since Hope comes *with God*, we have to position ourselves for the presence of God. Positioning ourselves begins with honesty, with ourselves and God, about our dissatisfaction.

We tend to look down on people who express dissatisfaction, particularly in the church. At best, we treat them as whiners. At worst, we consider their expression of dissatisfaction to be sinful.

In verbal and nonverbal ways, we communicate to the dissatisfied: "Your negative point of view clearly indicates you are not connected to God. If you were a *better Christian*, you would not be so dissatisfied."

We tell the dissatisfied that they don't have enough faith.

We treat them like a squeaky wheel.

We shun them as immature.

In doing so, we are revealing our ignorance of Scripture. In the Bible we can find example after example where dissatisfaction and faith coexist, where frustration with the way things are and a deep sense of Hope are beautiful friends.

That's what this book hopes to explore. Real Hope—*faithful confidence that God continues to author a story that moves us from vision to action*—is found on a path with a dissatisfaction trailhead. And that path has its location in a territory called *exile*.

## Hope Toolbox

- Before starting this book, how would you have defined hope? What do you like about your definition of hope? Now that you've read this chapter, in what ways does your previous definition of hope seem lacking (if any)?

- How would you describe the difference between Roody's outlook and Michelle's outlook? How would you describe the dissonance between the two stories? Why do you think some people are able to find Hope, while others struggle?   *Openess to God*
- Think of a time when you "cherished something with anticipation." What were the circumstances of that experience, and what was the result? If Hope is *faithful confidence that God continues to author a story that moves us from vision to action*, what implications might that have for you and your life?

# TWO

# EXILE

## *Life Without Hope*

Joseph, the biblical young man with the ostentatious, fabulous robe, involuntarily landed in a foreign land. It's not clear whether Joseph was oblivious to his many brothers' jealousy over a dad who played favorites or was gleefully pushing their buttons, but he barely avoided siblingcide when his brothers sold him into slavery.

Hello, Egypt!

Of course, Joseph—after some ups and downs—ended up being used by God to provide brilliant leadership through a multi-year famine. His brothers came begging for food; and the family that was, at that time, the entirety of the Hebrew race, dodged a starvation bullet and spent some happy years in a foreign land.

Then we lose the storyline for about four centuries. A couple significant factors have changed when we re-engage this family. First, they're clearly good at babymaking, as they've become a massive people group. Second, and in the "however" column, the Pharaohs have repurposed them into slaves working on their ambitious building programs. So even though Joseph's trip to Egypt might have felt like exile at first, it turned out to be a beautiful means of salvation for his family. But after the end of the famine and many, many generations, the Israelites found themselves living a reality that, to this day, is an archetype of suffering and displacement.

Living in squalor, under brutal overseers, doing backbreaking work, all in a desert land that is not your own. This was exile at its worst.

## MY MINI-EXILE

I experienced a mini-exile in a real and metaphorical desert a few years ago. I had a job that I thought I'd be in for the rest of my life, a job with an organization I loved in the deepest parts of my soul and self. My job had great meaning and provided everything I imagined a job could ever provide: purpose, friendships, influence, fun, opportunities for risk and creativity and making a difference in peoples' lives, and pretty decent financial comfort.

Then, through protracted pressure from a parent company CEO to become something we weren't (and something I wasn't), our merry band of revolutionaries got squished under a corporate thumb, broken up and sold in pieces. And I lost my job.

The reasons for my role's elimination made perfect business sense. But the actual process was fumbled in a way that left me feeling horribly diminished and instantly isolated (for example: my former coworkers—my friends—were expressly forbidden to have any contact with me out of fear that I would somehow mess up the still-pending sale of the company).

I don't want to be overly dramatic, and my pain in that season was—I realize—minor compared to the suffering of, say, a Haitian after the earthquake, or even one of many people I know who have lost children. But pain is pain, and mine was very real, very present and completely disorienting.

The anxiety and fear were almost overwhelming and I wondered if I might be on the verge of some sort of psychotic breakdown. I felt damaged and filleted and tossed aside. And the loneliness almost undid me.

In the worst low, I went to the desert. Really. I drove ninety minutes east of my home in San Diego to a funky cabin in the desert loaned to me by some saints from my church. I went for a week of silence, seeking separation from the screaming voices in my head and heart. I went seeking a nonoptional break from the voices on the Internet and my phone (the cabin had no cell reception or Internet access). I went to air out my emotions. Now, I'm a fairly easygoing guy, not practiced at understanding or interpreting intense emotions. And these were just too much to let roll off my back. They required processing. So I went to find God.

I had a tiny, undeveloped sliver of a thought in my mind, that it just might be possible I would find God waiting out there in that desert exile. I was right about that. But I didn't choose a self-imposed mini-exile thinking I would find Hope; that wasn't even on my radar. I was merely hoping that God might sit shiva with me, comourning my loss.

But.

Where God is, Hope is also. So when I bumped into God in the desert, Hope came as a part of the combo platter.

## EXILE AS THE CULTURE OF HOPE

I remember a grade school science project where we grew mold. This being a very scientific endeavor, we were actually comparing the various quantities of mold that grew on small pieces of cooked hamburger from a variety of restaurants.

We dropped the little burger bits into small round plastic containers called petri dishes. Each petri dish contained a mysterious semiclear gelatin that we learned to call a "culture." The culture provided a suspended source of moisture and a pillow of immobilization.

That's the role of exile in our search for Hope, because Hope comes to us in the midst of exile.

Thomas à Kempis, in his classic book *The Imitation of Christ*, writes a line said to be a favorite of Vincent Van Gogh: "If you want to persevere and make spiritual progress, look upon yourself as an exile and a pilgrim on this earth."[1]

Exile is, in a formal sense, the banishment or forced removal from one's native country. But exile can take nongeographic forms. If we reframe exile as any time we experience relational banishment, metaphorical deportation, or isolation from a native connectivity, we start to see exiles little and large in all our lives.

My trip to the California desert wasn't technically exile because I chose it; but there's no question that I was experiencing a forced isolation—an exile—from people and dreams and security and future plans.

That place of separation from everything we know, all we long to be a part of, even all we take for granted, plucks us out of the here and now and drops us into a place of limbo. Exile always feels like an uneasy in-between. Exile rips open an empty space in our souls, and that loud sucking sound is the vacuum of longing for both what was and what we expected would be.

Exile = not home.

Have you experienced this? Most of us have, at one time or another. And if you haven't, it's likely you will. Maybe it's possible to live wonderfully hopeful lives without exile, but I'm suggesting that most (maybe all?) Hope-filled lives first encounter Hope in exile.

Remember the Jewish slaves, painfully erecting pyramids and sphinxes and such? Here's how their feelings about their exile got expressed: "The Israelites groaned in their slavery and cried out" (Exodus 2:23).

Groaning. That's a great word for the result of exile in our lives.

We *groan* when the internal pain (physical or otherwise) is too much to bear. We *groan* when our interior feelings of pain and isolation and lostness are so overwhelming that they demand an audible response, but there are simply no words.

Groaning isn't even a cry for help. It's just a gut sound, chock-full of complex meaning.

But here's the counterintuitive and biblical truth: exile is the culture in which we begin our journey to Hope. Hope—the transformative, life-giving kind, not the wishful thinking variety—is rarely found in places of ease. Hope doesn't cozy up well with comfort. Hope isn't snuggle buddies with affluence or good times.

Nope. Instead, we see Hope over and over again in Scripture *arriving like God's whisper* in a groaning place of exile.

## OUT OF THE FRYING PAN, INTO THE DESERT

There's no question that the exodus is one of the most central stories in the Jewish narrative, and also one of the most important in the arc of the Christian Bible. When we Christians practice Communion, or what's called the Eucharist by some, we're not only reenacting the Last Supper Jesus celebrated with his disciples, we're directly connecting with the Jewish celebration of Passover. And that takes our own storyline directly back to the exodus.

In Exodus 12:26-27, Moses tells the people, "And when your children ask you, 'What does this ceremony mean to you?' then tell them, 'It is the Passover sacrifice to the LORD, who passed over the houses of the Israelites in Egypt and spared our homes when he struck down the Egyptians.'"

But we know the whole storyline; we know about the eventual arrival in the Promised Land.

Think of the experience of the exodus from the perspective of the enslaved Hebrew people. After generations of brutal treatment in their Egyptian exile—the only life every single Jewish man, woman and child had ever known—God provides a way out. The open pathway leads smack dab through the soggy bottom of the Red Sea (I can't help but picture Cecil B. DeMille's sea walls of gelatin!).

Arriving on the other side, and watching those temporary, massive sea walls crash down on their pursuers hoping to re-enslave them, must have created an overwhelming experiential emotion: *We are free!*

*Our slavery is behind us! God has delivered us out of exile.*

Except.

They wandered in the desert for another forty years. With an average lifespan somewhere in the thirties, an entire generation of Red Sea walkers never made it to the Promised Land. The Egyptian exile had a generation-long coda, an appendix of desert camping, complaining and discouragement. We are quick to look down on the whiners who cried out to Moses,

> Was it because there were no graves in Egypt that you brought us to the desert to die? What have you done to us by bringing us out of Egypt? Didn't we say to you in Egypt, "Leave us alone; let us serve the Egyptians"? It would have been better for us to serve the Egyptians than to die in the desert! (Exodus 14:11-12)

But I think it's pretty likely I would have been crying along with everyone else; or, at the least, passive-aggressively thinking the same thing, dismissing Moses as a lousy leader.

And a short while later, when Moses makes his solo ascent up Mount Sinai—lingering for what seems, from an "in the valley below" perspective, just *way too long*—the Hebrew people again cry out to Aaron, Moses' brother, "Come, make us gods who will go before us. As for this fellow Moses who brought us up out of Egypt, we don't know what has happened to him" (Exodus 32:1).

As a youth worker with more than thirty years of teaching teenagers, I have often used this story as an example of shallow commitment, mocking Aaron's capitulation and the easy-to-parody absurdity of Aaron's later explanation to Moses: *I don't know what happened! The people complained, and we tossed their gold jewelry in the fire, and out walked this little gold cow!*

Middle schoolers think that story is pretty funny, especially the way I tell it. Easy laughs. Point made. Score: Self-righteous, 1. Those without conviction, 0.

But hold on a minute there. I'm no different than those who begged for an adjustment in what must have felt like a completely botched rescue operation. Certainly, I know people—living saints—who stay firm in faith and patience while the rescue from their exile continues to be put on hold. But I can't count my story (or patience) among them.

During my own mini-exile described earlier, one of my primary thoughts was to leave behind any ministry role that could ever again hurt me. I was idolizing safety. I was giving in to hardcore cynicism, buffering myself from potential pain. In fact, I'm sure the examples of crying out for a different or new god are countless in my life. I might not word it the same way as the Hebrew people did, but the desires of my heart have many times been the same.

And I've lost count of the number of my friends, many who were actively involved in ministry roles, who have ebbed away from any meaningful moorings of an explicitly Christian faith. Some of these fadings were the result of an unsatisfying or unsustainable set of beliefs, but more of them were the result of the weariness of exile.

Hear me out: I'm not suggesting that those friends of mine are particularly weak or shallow. I'm suggesting that we are *all* particularly weak and shallow, and my current status as someone who still holds to Christian faith has very little to do with my efforts or the quality of my character.

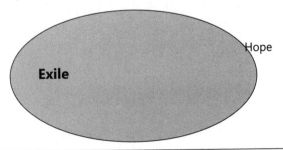

**Figure 2.1**

Be honest: exile stinks. And a big part of why it's so distasteful is that it usually lasts for a while. Deep down, we all know that we're weak, and we simply don't have the power within us to remain true.

Whatever my convictions and beliefs might be during the good times, I'm a wimp when things turn sour. And, come on, be honest enough to admit that you might be the same way.

We might represent the relationship of exile and Hope this way:

Hope is out there, and even has one leg of its leading letter dangling in, hinting at possibilities. But exile, when we're in it, feels so massive and monolithic that Hope seems very, very far off. Almost impossibly remote.

## EXILIC INTENSIFIERS

The Hebrew people in the desert had their own set of unique, contextual circumstances that exacerbated the weariness of their exile (including the fact that they were in the desert . . . *and* they'd been slaves . . . *and* they were still in the desert due to their own choices, forty years *after* their rescue!). But we also have our own unique, contextual circumstances magnifying our experiences of exile.

Our exilic intensifiers are usually less visceral than actual deserts and the literal whip of an overseer. Ours are cultural, primarily, but they are extremely effective at strong-arming us into impatience.

First, we live in a *culture of information*. You've likely read or heard these sorts of details elsewhere, but the amount of knowledge and information that exists in the world is said to double roughly every eight years. That's insane. It's an absurd understatement to call it "exponential" growth. By implication, that means that the percentage of existing knowledge that you personally know is decreasing exponentially!

But an enormous additional dimension to this steep increase in information is the ease at which we can access all of it. No longer are these mountains of knowledge and information protected in musty libraries and hidden in government laboratories: almost all knowledge is accessible to us with the click of a mouse, or increasingly, the touch of a thumb on our mobile platforms. Unless you live "off the grid" (and

I doubt too many from that tribe will be reading this book), information is in your face constantly, whether you want it or not.

What does that have to do with exile? Well, once we learn, deep in our subconscious, that everything we could ever want to know is available at all times, we come to expect that the answer to any significant challenge is similarly accessible, as if God were Siri on an iPhone.

We are constantly steeping in a hot water of accessible information, and that erodes our ability to withstand the rigors of exile. We want it over—NOW! And we're constantly told that our problems (the cause of our exile) are fixable if we will simply follow five easy steps (or three, or eight or whatever the most recent blog prescribes).

My guess is that the Hebrew people in the desert, after years of slavery, were *much more* attuned to answers not being readily available. That sorta reframes their frustration with the apparently lost Moses.

Second, and related to the culture of information, we're living in a *culture of immediacy*. Not only is all knowledge and information available (at least more of it than we could ever use), it's all available at this moment, as are goods and services. It's all accessible anytime, anywhere.

When we have to *wait* for something these days, it automatically feels foreign or antiquated.

If you're old enough, you might remember when shaking a Polaroid picture for a full minute, waiting for the image to be realized on the strange plasticky surface of the spewed-out photograph, was the pinnacle of speed. Now, we get twitchy when someone doesn't respond to our text message within seconds. Teenagers and young adults (who are native to this culture, while us older folks are immigrants) regularly add a layer of meaning to a delayed text response: the other person is avoiding me, or must be upset, or doesn't like me.

When so many things in our world are immediate, we find it insanely difficult to possess any sense of patience. Waiting for Hope to show up in the midst of exile is a hardcore practice of patience. And without patience, our exile often results in complete hopelessness, and even an inability to notice when Hope peeks around the corner.

Finally, we also live in a *culture of disposability*.

The easiest place to see this is our relationships with hard goods, from contact lenses to mobile phones to car leases. Even the laptop I'm typing on right now—a very nice upgraded MacBook Air—has a "planned" or "built-in obsolescence" of about eighteen months (of course, Apple is brilliant at promoting and exploiting this). And what should I do with this fairly expensive and originally cutting-edge computer when I *need* the new version for whatever reason? Really, I might be able to get twenty or thirty bucks for it on Craigslist; but it won't be much more than a formerly useful paperweight.

Another easy-to-grasp example for our relationship with technology: computer printers. Several years ago now, the printer industry went through a major reorientation of change-or-die proportions. Printers became cheap and disposable when printer manufacturers realized they could make more money from ink sales if they got people to buy low priced printers that required disposable ink cartridges. I purchased the printer that sits on my desk for the best price possible: FREE! But I spend more money annually on the stupid ink cartridges (which are also disposable, by the way) than I spend on car tires!

The culture of disposability, though, is *way* more far-reaching than the lack of permanence with respect to our technology hard goods. Disposability has become the norm for most things (unless they're seen as a commodity with appreciating value, which is not the world most people live in). In this reality, careers are disposable, and relationships are disposable, and experiences (merely another item to be consumed for their temporary satisfaction) and even beliefs are disposable.

When we become so deeply skilled and practiced at a lifestyle and mindset that embraces the disposability of all things, exile becomes . . . well . . . impossible to bear! All efforts and thoughts immediately get directed toward, *I must get out of this at this second; I must dispose of this exile; surely this exile has a planned obsolescence.*

I'm not an anti-culture guy. I'm not pining for "the good old days." Whenever I watch a movie or read a book set in a long-ago time period, particularly something like the Middle Ages or even something like feudal England, I regularly think to myself, "I'm so glad I didn't live then!" I like the Internet. I'm a fan of my phone apps. And you'll never find me complaining about the fact that I don't have to stop for directions anymore.

Culture is our collectively developed ways of living and interacting and valuing, and every culture has upsides and downsides. So my point in this section is not to paint culture as a great evil that proves how hellbound and godless this generation is. Uh-uh. I'm more hopeful than that.

But we have to admit that our cultural realities—including the cultures of information, immediacy and disposability—create particular and unique challenges for us when it comes to experiences of exile. And we *all* have experiences of exile. (Remember, that's a good thing, because Hope comes to us while we're in exile.)

## THE FLYWHEEL OF HOPE

In the consulting work I do with churches and other ministries, I'm usually brought in to help foment change. Most organizations (churches, businesses, nonprofits, civic groups) strive toward a wrongheaded ideal of stability. The incorrect thinking is, *If we can get to a place of success* (however that is defined), *and put the systems and people in place who can help us stay there, we can ride this wave for a long time.*

Problem is, that never works. Never.

Stability is, in my observation, one of the worst places to be as an organization because it's the moment-in-time tipping point (it's never a protracted season in reality) of moving from growing to aging. Stability is the beginning of the slide to death.

I try to help organizations understand that only with a "flywheel of change" can they maintain vibrancy. And, counterintuitively, that process of ongoing change has to be initiated *prior to* arrival at stability (thereby staving off stability, and allowing the organization to stay in what at least one organizational theorist calls "prime").[2]

I love the metaphor of a flywheel, and think it's also helpful for us in understanding the potential of Hope arriving in exile.

A flywheel is an energy reservoir. It's a momentum repository. Once a flywheel is turning, it's very easy to maintain its movement. Of course, it will wind down and eventually stop if ignored; but the effort involved in keeping it moving is not significant.

A helpful visual of a flywheel is the original flywheel: the millstone. A millstone is a large stone disc, spinning on an axis. Millstones were used in—you guessed it—mills. Before electricity, millstones did the work of grinding grain (between the spinning millstone and a stationary "bedstone").

Getting a big, heavy millstone started is hard work—those first few pushes are backbreaking work. But once the millstone is moving, the donkey or humans doing the pushing simply have to walk in a circle. Easy peasy.

In the same sense, a life of true Hope is very much like a millstone—a big heavy flywheel. Once Hope drops into our lives (more on that part later), it's much more than a passing whimsy of fleeting happiness. Hope swells, invades, pushing away our whining, melancholy and morose, and sets up shop in our hearts.

And here's the good news for those in exile: the very experience of exile—loneliness, isolation, discouragement, confusion, lostness—is exactly the right place for those first few hard pushes on the flywheel of Hope. Our pushes don't *create* Hope, but they position us for the influx of Hope that comes from Jesus.

In short: the first push is an articulation of our dissatisfaction; and the second push is an honest cry out to God. But neither of those pushes is as simple and easy as it sounds.

# HOPE TOOLBOX

- Think of the worst experience of exile you've been through in your life.
  Don't worry about comparing it to others'—that's not helpful. What
  brought about the exile? What did you lose in your exile? What
  feelings do you remember from that time? *Hope*
  *discouragement, doubt, lack of faith*
- What's an exile you're currently experiencing (or, if you really can't
  think of one, what was the most recent)? You might have an inner voice
  telling you "Stop being a whiner, it's not that bad!" Ignore that voice.
  Whether your loss or separation has external markers (loss of a job or
  relationship, betrayal, financial struggle) or is completely internal (like
  the loss of a dream), put some words to it. There is *absolutely no shame*
  in this. *death, sickness — tired, barely coping*

- Reflect on this question while resisting the temptation to give a
  churchy answer: Where is God during exile? Where does it *feel* like
  God is? *In the midst*         *far away at times*

# THREE

# IDENTIFYING HOPE'S ENEMIES

We all experience exile. And we all want Hope. So if I'm correct that Hope comes to us in exile, why does Hope seem so elusive?

When I was about ten years old, my family stopped by my dad's office on our way to some sort of church gathering. I distinctly remember what I was wearing that day (brace yourself): white dress slacks, white shoes and a white belt, nicely accented with a maroon dress shirt. I was the perfect picture of a 1970s preteen, dressed to impress.

My dad's office was in the middle of some woods, but there was a subdivision being built nearby; and what preteen boy can resist the pull of exploring a construction site? I had a friend with me that day, and we asked if we could explore while my parents did whatever it was they needed to do. My mom's cautious approval came with a clear directive: "Only if you *do not* get dirty."

Off we went, fully intending to keep the white pants white.

On the construction worksite, we found a mostly frozen-over mini-pond of awesomeness. A muddy area had apparently been partially flooded during the winter months, and was actively thawing on this springtime Detroit Sunday. There was a large ice island in the middle, with a bit of a causeway leading to it. Of course, I quickly found myself planting a stake (literally) in the ice island and claiming it for the motherland. Only then, amidst the revelry of conquering, did I notice that the causeway had disintegrated after I'd crossed to the island.

I panicked. *Do I stay out here on this ice island, maintaining the whiteness of my clothes and the purity of my intentions to behave as instructed?* What other options were there? I didn't *want* to be on the island. But both staying put and doing anything else seemed to only have tragic outcomes.

I felt a shift under my feet. At first I thought the island might be breaking into pieces; but instead, the whole berg was slowly sinking under my weight. Brown, muddy water started flowing over the edges toward my outpost in the middle.

My friend was trying to help, I'm sure. But when he pushed a large, floating wooden door toward me and yelled, "Use this as a raft," neither of us were thinking very clearly. Needless to say, I took a mud bath that day.

I was on that exilic island by my own doing (our exiles are sometimes, though not always, due to our own choices). But I quickly wanted out. In my panic, I jumped for a promise that couldn't deliver.

When we're in the midst of the pain of exile, Hope can seem impossible. We're desperate, and therefore highly susceptible to the lies our culture tells us about how to extricate ourselves.

Really, since an influx of Hope is about opening ourselves up to the influx of God's presence, the enemies of Hope are wolves in sheep's clothing, encouraging us to retain control.

We humans have developed myriad ways of keeping God at arm's length during our times of exile. We buy into these false solutions because we believe they're less risky than completely opening up to a faithful confidence that God continues to author the story.

## HOPE ENEMY #1: BUSYNESS AS USUAL

Nothing keeps Hope at a distance more often and more quickly than the distraction of busyness. Jesus is interested in our journey, not merely our destination; and God seems to be very, very content with slow (or, at least, what seems slow to us). But we often clutter up our lives with busyness, which relegates positioning ourselves for Hope to the bottom of our to-do lists.

Paraphrasing the apostle Paul, I'm the chief sinner in this area. I make myself busy for all sorts of reasons, but very few of them are helpful or healthy. I feel important when I'm busy. I feel needed, and necessary. It's imbecilic how significant I feel while spinning plates.

My teenage son, Max, is one of the true joys of my life. He's an amazing young man, just now stepping into manhood. He's sensitive and empathetic and gentle, full of creativity and humor, and passionate about justice. But Max regularly drives us nuts in his apparent inability to focus beyond the moment. He forgets what we asked him to do, and is easily distracted.

This behavior is sometimes a challenge for Max's teachers also. I remember a few years ago, when his teacher—a tenderhearted saint of a woman, and a highly gifted teacher—reconfigured my entire view of Max's apparent lack of care for whatever goal seems pressing to all but him. She and I were sharing, in passing, about some deadline he'd missed or item he'd misplaced, and she uttered this simple little insight into living: "Well, we all have something to learn from Max about being present in every moment."

The most hopeful people are never frenetic. I'm not suggesting they're passive (because Hope is active). But they know how to breathe. They're practiced in the art of waiting, and noticing, and listening.

Busyness, ultimately, is an embracing of the lie that we control our own destinies. At best, busyness makes God an item on the to-do list, and the Hope that God wants to bring into our exile is suffocated.

## HOPE ENEMY #2: LAZY EYE

A number of years ago, a fellow youth worker gave me a T-shirt that

*[handwritten marginal note: I am looking for a slightly different pace to my life.]*

said, in bold letters: *I don't have a short attention span, I just . . . Oh look, a squirrel!*

Maybe I'm only writing to myself here, but, wow, some of us are easily distracted.

The psalmist wrote, "I lift up my eyes to the mountains—where does my help come from? My help comes from the LORD, the Maker of heaven and earth" (Psalm 121:1-2). Honestly, there's a lot of stuff to look at in the mountains! In my exile, I might lift my eyes up to the mountains looking for rescue and Hope, but my attention immediately starts to flit all over the place.

Put yourself in Elijah's sandals for a moment. After Elijah's amazing showdown with the prophets of Baal (1 Kings 18) where God torched a water-soaked offering in response to Elijah's prayer that God's power would be shown, he was running for his life. Jezebel was *not pleased* that her prophets had been proved impotent, and subsequently killed. First Kings 19 tells us:

> Elijah was afraid and ran for his life. When he came to Beer-sheba in Judah, he left his servant there, while he himself went a day's journey into the wilderness. He came to a broom bush, sat down under it and prayed that he might die. "I have had enough, LORD," he said. "Take my life; I am no better than my ancestors." Then he lay down under the bush and fell asleep. (1 Kings 19:3-5)

Sounds like Elijah is entering into a bit of exile, right? But God shows up in Elijah's exile. It's a famous passage:

> The LORD said, "Go out and stand on the mountain in the presence of the LORD, for the LORD is about to pass by."
>
> Then a great and powerful wind tore the mountains apart and shattered the rocks before the LORD, but the LORD was not in the wind. After the wind there was an earthquake, but the LORD

*[handwritten margin note: God comes to us in our time of need—our exile.]*

was not in the earthquake. After the earthquake came a fire, but the LORD was not in the fire. And after the fire came a gentle whisper. When Elijah heard it, he pulled his cloak over his face and went out and stood at the mouth of the cave. (1 Kings 19:11-13)

Awesome story. But here's my problem: I would have been completely and utterly focused on the wind that tore the mountains apart, and the earthquake, and the fire. I'm so easily distracted by opportunity and threats and temptations and rewards and daydreams that I'm pretty sure I would have completely missed the gentle whisper of God's presence. In that whisper, and the conversation that follows, Elijah's Hope is restored and his short exile ended.

Making space for Hope's arrival isn't simple for those of us who are easily distracted. It takes focus and concentration and faith that the Source of Hope is going to show up.

Those distractions can be bad things, of course: threats and pressures and accommodations. But they're often compromises, or good things, or even seemingly great things, that steal our imagination and keep us off course, hopelessly stuck in exile.

## HOPE ENEMY #3: THE HAPPY POLICE

As someone who's spent thirty-three years in youth ministry—the majority of that with middle schoolers—I've certainly experienced my share of embarrassing ministry moments.[1] But most of them have centered on malapropisms or other verbal blunders. Only a handful of times have I experienced the sort of embarrassment that made me angry.

I was a rookie junior high pastor at a large church in the Midwest. Our aging outreach and evangelism pastor, a wonderful and gracious man, held massive sway in the church due to his history and alignment with the church's values. So when he told us all about an "opportunity" to host an event to evangelize business leaders in our community, the other pastors went along with it.

The event centered on bringing in a known motivational speaker who happened to be a Jesus-y person in private. Though no one on our leadership would have used the term, we were going to employ the classic bait and switch approach to evangelism. Youth ministries have done this for decades, so I'm quite familiar with it ("Come for the haunted house! Then we'll trap you in a room and scare you into heaven!"). Full disclosure: I wasn't that uncomfortable, at that time in my maturity and spiritual journey, with a bait and switch. But I still felt it should be handled with a bit of finesse.

I'll call the motivational speaker Bobby W. Clark, which is not his real name. He has long since passed away, so my purpose in telling this story is not to denigrate the name of a dead privately Christian motivational speaker but to illustrate our confusion about Hope and optimism.

The W in his name—whatever it stood for on his birth certificate—was part of his schtick, and he went by Bobby "Wonderful" Clark. As I would come to find out, he was a very minor celebrity who'd been working the corporate pump-'em-up circuit longer than I'd been alive.

The plan for our church's event was this: Host a nice dinner in a hotel ballroom, with the opportunity to hear this Wonderful business speaker. Guilt our church members, particularly those with influential business roles, to invite (persuade) multitudes of business associates to attend. Slip in the gospel. And, BAM, more business leaders in heaven!

I wasn't in business. I didn't have business associates. But my wife did. She was a low-level but professional employee at a natural gas trading company (yes, fodder for lots of jokes about "natural gas" in my junior high ministry world). So I did what I thought I was supposed to do: I pressured my wife to pressure her business associates to attend this Wonderful opportunity. And a few of them, very reluctantly, came along.

The food was good enough. But good old Bobby: well, let's just say the operative word in that phrase was "old." Seriously, I think he came out of retirement for this gig so he could afford another golf trip to Florida or something.

I have two extremely groan-worthy memories of that night, even though it was well over twenty years ago. The first of those memories was the root of my anger-tinged embarrassment. Bobby's bait and switch was just the worst I'd ever seen. After offering literally three minutes of business-y clichés (shorter than his introduction by the evening's emcee), he launched into a horribly hackneyed and manipulative presentation of the gospel complete with a simultaneously high pressure *and* confusing prayer of salvation. My wife and I were both horrified. Our church had traded on her friendships with colleagues and given them nothing more than a caricature of their worst assumptions of what the night might contain.

But my second memory of that night is the reason I tell this story. Bobby had a signature move. Really. Like, no one else could do that move without someone saying, "Hey, that's Bobby W. Clark's move!" I think there's a little twisted part of me that admires anyone who has a signature move. Except . . .

Bobby's signature move went like this: he would say something like, "I'm Bobby Clark, and I'm here to tell you that *Life is Wonderful!*" When Bobby said this last phrase (which he said multiple times during his talk) he would kick one long leg (he was really tall) high in the air. It was a bit startling the first time you saw it since it's not a common movement for a man in a business suit.

But remember, Bobby was *old*. And his signature move required a bit more coordination—even athleticism—than Bobby possessed by that night. The first time he attempted the kick, right after he was introduced, there was a long pause between "I'm here to tell you that life is . . ." and "wonderful," with the leg kick. It was like he had to coax his body into action. On his first attempt, he only got his leg partially up in the air, and stumbled to the side. The audience silently willed him to move on, but he was *not* going to leave without executing his signature move.

It took him *three tries*. But he got it. And with newly reinvigorated confidence, Bobby busted out the leg kick three or four more times during his talk, rivaling even the Rockettes.

Mr. Wonderful was selling us a very, very subtle lie that even he likely had no awareness of: *pretending you're happy makes life better.*

The core of Bobby's motivational schtick was simple: choose to be happy, select the perky option, pretend that nothing's wrong, ignore your pain, and you'll be more productive and garner success.

I like happiness. Nothing wrong with that. And I generally agree with the sentiment that Life is Wonderful. But leg kicks and smiles won't close the gap between the life I'm living and the life I long for.

Several years ago now, a little book called *The Secret* sold millions and became a runaway *New York Times* bestseller. The essence of *The Secret* was simply this: visualize the positive future you want for yourself, claim it to be true, and it will come to be.

And while Christians might have chafed at that message (for good reasons), we have all too often taught a version of the same. Sure, we spread a little Jesus mayo on that self-actualization sandwich. We say it's God who brings the blessing, not our own efforts at positive thinking. But really, what we've often taught (and thought) is only a tiny shade different: our positive thinking allows God to bless us.

Of course, part of the problem is that we use the word *hope* for all sorts of things and in all sorts of ways that are not the same as faithful confidence that God continues to author a story that moves us from vision to action.

*I hope I get that job.*
*I hope my team wins this big game.*
*I hope the weather is good tomorrow.*

I have nothing against those expressions of the word *hope*. I'm sure I use them all the time. In fact, I'm very much an optimist. And I must, to some extent, believe that optimism is a good and healthy perspective. I know I'd much rather surround myself with people who see possibilities and silver linings than people who, like Eeyore the donkey from Winnie the Pooh, see only the negatives and believe we're doomed.

So let's be clear about this: optimism is wonderful. I'm a fan of optimism.

But optimism is *not* the same thing as life-giving Hope.

In high school, my parents grew weary of the multiple ways I was finding to abuse their Volkswagen Bug. They issued an ultimatum that I would lose driving privileges for a time if I had another infraction. So I totally panicked when my buddies thought it was hilarious to somehow completely fill the inside of the car—all the way to the roof—with the tiny styrofoam pellets you find in bean bag chairs (or could find, back then).

I drove around the church parking lot with the doors open, allowing the styro-bits to create their own weather pattern. Then I pumped quarter after quarter into a self-serve car wash's industrial vacuum, making sure I sucked up every single last piece of evidence.

All was well, I convinced myself, for a few weeks. Then the first cold day of the fall arrived, unfortunately, when my dad and I were in the car together. The windows fogged up. As we drove down a major road, my dad reached over and turned on the defrost fan. On a Volkswagen Bug, the windshield is almost vertical, and the defrost vents point straight up. How was I to know that they were filled with thousands of patient, hiding, styrofoam balls, which engulfed the inside of the car with a blinding snowstorm?

You can convince yourself for a while that optimism will get you where you want to go. But eventually, optimism will be found out as limited. Optimism will fall short. Optimism's great for a short sprint, but Hope is needed for a lifetime journey.

## HOPE ENEMY #4: BUCKETS OF GOLD

Here's a (tongue-in-cheek) suggestion for how you can keep Hope at bay: win the lottery or in some other way stumble into a cornucopia of resources. Even though Hope rearranges our interior lives and de-fangs our anxieties, Hope still implies that there's some *longing*, some *waiting* some *desperation* for something still out there! Our desire for wealth and resources is rooted in the lie that they will eliminate our longings. Remember Romans 8:22-23:

> We know that the whole creation has been groaning as in the pains of childbirth right up to the present time. Not only so, but we ourselves, who have the firstfruits of the Spirit, groan in-wardly as we wait eagerly for our adoption, the redemption of our bodies.

I have participated in roughly fifty National Youth Workers Con-ventions in the United States over the years, a large-scale gathering of church youth workers. Those youth workers are my tribe, and I love them to death. I've also participated in roughly twenty or so Conven-cións Internacional Líderes Juvenil, the Spanish-language version of the same event, in Buenos Aires, Argentina, and Guatemala City, Guatemala (and more recently in Orlando).

The format of the two events is almost identical. Sometimes the visuals and themes have been shared or repurposed. Even the size (somewhere between two and three thousand) is the same. The only initial indicator that they're different events is the obvious one: lan-guage.

But spending time at so many of them, I started to pick up another, more subtle difference. The American (English-language) conven-tions are fantastic, but there's an undercurrent of pervasive com-plaining and frustration. The Latin events, instead, have an under-current of pervasive Hope and joy.

Reflecting on this, I saw one glaring contrast: the Latin American youth workers have nothing—no budgets, no paid youth workers, no training, no support. They have nothing but a sense of calling and "Christ in [them], the hope of glory" (Colossians 1:27).

Being well resourced (whether that's money or other resources) easily seduces us into believing that resources are the source of our salvation. We say to ourselves, "Well, sure, money can't buy you everything; but it sure would give me options for getting out of this mess."

If you want to receive Hope, in exile or post-exile, learn to rejoice in your lack of resources.

## HOPE ENEMY #5: ALL SYSTEMS ARE GO!

I like to blame this Hope enemy on Henry Ford, the godfather of the assembly line. But he was merely taking to a logical conclusion the values of his time. Mechanize something—turn it into a predictable assembly line with minimal variations—and the outcomes will be predictable. Somewhere along the line, "predictable" became synonymous with "better."

Technique (the word theologian Walter Brueggemann uses[2]) is counterintuitively destructive to Hope. I'll be proposing a model for receiving and experiencing Hope in this book, but I trust you won't misread it as a technique. And it's really not as predictably linear as I'll make it sound; we often loop through it multiple times, at multiple points in our lives.

There are fantastic pockets of resistance to our obsessions with fast and systematized and predictable, such as etsy.com or the Slow Food movement. But sadly, much of our popular theology and Christian practice is still being informed by an assembly-line mentality. We love to reduce the mystery of being a Christ-follower into quick and easy steps:

8 steps to being a disciple

10 steps to the perfect Christian marriage

142 steps to effectively parenting the perfect child

Our best techniques will never create Hope. Deep Hope is only found in Christ. Paul states this emphatically in 1 Timothy 4:9-10: "This is a trustworthy saying that deserves full acceptance. That is why we labor and strive, because we have put our hope in the living God, who is the Savior of all people, and especially of those who believe."

## HOPE ENEMY #6: THE OPPOSITE OF HOPE

One of the ways I think of Hope is to see it as the opposite of cynicism. Hope and cynicism cannot coexist. They're not two sides of the same coin, or yin and yang; they're mutually exclusive of one another.

Cynicism says, "I can't change," or "We aren't capable of change," or "There's no way this situation will ever change." Cynicism is the voice of resistance that keeps us from what's possible. Cynicism encourages us to keep a tight grip on control. Cynicism dismisses faith as childish. And it completely closes the doors and windows to the potential arrival of Hope, diminishing Hope with labels like "utopian," "idealistic" and "Pollyanna."

Cynics are risk averse. They stay aloof and disengaged (from others *and* themselves) as a means of pain avoidance. Connecting with others or investing our emotions or feeling deeply might, in the mind of a cynic, lead to hurt and suffering, which would distance them from the good life as they imagine it. Cynics set the bar too low in order to avoid disappointment.

Think of it this way: it's tough to find a cynical child. Children are naturally hopeful. They believe that anything truly is possible. They don't merely *believe* that things could be better, they have faith—belief in action—that the world can be a better place. They have faith in themselves, faith in others, and (assuming a childlike Christian worldview) faith in God to bring about good.

But somewhere during our teenage and young adult years, most of us develop a hearty intimacy with cynicism. We've been exposed to too much false advertising. We've seen too many people promise change and not deliver. We've tried to apply optimism to our own insufficiencies and found the results lacking. We've wrestled with the goodness of God, and we find the pervasive pain and struggle of so many in the world to feel capricious, or even evidence of a God who doesn't care enough about his creation to intervene.

Maybe it's self-protection, this cynical bent that so many of us embrace. It's easier to be a cynic than to put hope on the line yet again. It's safer to assume nothing can or will change; then our hopes won't be dashed once again.

And it doesn't help that cynicism is often cherished as a hipster outlook, the semi-comical perspective of a realist. Yeah, that's the heart of it: when pressed, we pass off our cynicism as realism. "I'm not a pessimist, I'm just a realist; and I realistically *know* that nothing ever changes, including people."

Thanks for that, Eeyore.

## BACK TO THE MILLSTONE

Now we've established a working definition of Hope as *faithful confidence that God continues to author a story that moves us from vision to action*, substantively different from optimism or wishful thinking. And we've identified that we all experience exiles, big and small. I've suggested that Hope is a gift that comes to us, with the presence of God, breaking into our hopeless exiles. And we've talked about six mindsets or practices (Hope enemies) that counterintuitively keep us stuck in exile—I say they're counterintuitive because we're told, and we wrongly believe, that those mindsets and practices will ease our pain.

But there *are* a few practices (not a program or a method, and not a system) that help us lift our eyes to the mountains where our help comes from. These practices—the first few pushes on the heavy millstone—position us, open us up, for the influx of Hope that God passionately wants to bring. Those practices are: honesty with ourselves, honest cries to God and holding on to faith through our fears. That's where we're headed next.

# Hope Toolbox

- One of the Hope enemies—the happy police—is so prevalent and dominant in America that it has very much leaked into our churches and our theology. In what ways do you see this playing out in your experience? Where do you see or experience pressure to "just be happy"?

- As you read the six enemies of Hope, which one struck a chord with you the most? Why is that Hope enemy a particular danger for you?

- Prayerfully name that Hope enemy and consider its impact on you. Put some words to how you *feel* about that Hope enemy, and ask that God would give you wisdom to discern its lies.

FOUR

# POSITIONING FOR HOPE

*Honesty with Ourselves*

When I was a high school student, I went on a wilderness trip with my church. It was one of the smaller trips offered in my extremely active youth group, and only a handful of us traveled from the Detroit suburbs to Montreat, North Carolina, where we joined up with dozens of other teenagers from other churches for ten days in the Appalachian Mountains, backpacking, mountain climbing and canoeing.

The several dozen students on the trip were split into teams, and I found myself on a team with no one else from my church group. In a sort of Christianized version of Outward Bound, we were pushed to the very limit of our capabilities and capacities, carrying everything we needed on our backs and unavoidably learning to rely on the teamwork of other teenagers who certainly covered a wide gamut in their strengths, attitudes and annoying traits.

After a handful of days on the trail, we awoke to be told (by the one adult leader, who we were also just getting to know) that she was leaving us for the day and we'd be on our own. She pulled out the orienteering map we'd only learned to use in the past few days, plopped her pointer finger down and said, "We're here." She moved her finger across countless wavy lines indicating increases and decreases in elevation. "And you need to be here by tonight. I'll be waiting for you. Choose a leader and have a great day!"

I have a very vivid memory of our adult leader standing up (she was wearing blue jean overalls and monstrous hiking boots), turning her back to us and casually walking away, disappearing into thick under-growth within seconds.

None of us had uttered a single word the entire time Martha Sue was speaking. At least half of the group of ten had our mouths hanging wide open, still in shock and disbelief. I don't remember the first words spoken, but I'm pretty sure they weren't hopeful words uttered in con-fidence. Whatever we said, we were all thinking, "We're just kids! And our leader—the adult who's supposed to be responsible for us—just left us only-God-knows-where in the middle of Appalachia."

Nervous, but trying to talk each other into courage, we finished breakfast, packed our sleeping bags and chose a leader for the day. The leader did a bit of rookie orienteering on the map and pointed down a path: "That way!"

Well, we knew *that much*. But we set off, now in high spirits about our unquestionable superiority, both as teenagers and as wilderness authorities. Our steps were quick and full of pep, and our chatter was high-spirited and nonstop.

Until the trail started to fade.

As the afternoon drained, we found ourselves bushwhacking (we actually had machetes for this purpose, I think—but maybe that's a revisionist memory . . . did they really give machetes to teenagers then leave them alone?). Part of this struggle still felt like an aspect of the adventure. But it was hard work, painful (thin, springy branches were constantly whipping us) and slow going.

We rechecked the map over and over again, and were buoyed by our complete confidence that our destination was *just on the other side* of this semipenetrable thicket.

As the sun began to set (we were *way* behind schedule), we finally burst through the thickest of the choking plants into a glorious clearing, fully expecting Martha Sue to be waiting with a giant grin of approval on her face.

Nope. The only thing awaiting us was a massive stone wall. A steep cliff.

We didn't see the cliff wall on our map (it should have been a bunch of elevation lines really close together). Disoriented, we concluded the map was wrong (rather than that we were in the wrong place or reading the map incorrectly) and searched for an easy way *around* the cliff.

Scouts went out in both directions, certain we would find a gentler incline with which to complete what we knew were only the dozen or two remaining forward yards of our day. But an hour later the scouts returned to the rest of us huddling in the dark, revealing to us that there was no other way around—it was a wall in both directions. (Remember: this was before cell phones and GPS.)

The gap between *here* and *there* was—quite literally—less than fifty feet laterally. But that nasty vertical was making the gap impossible. We were SO CLOSE! We could sense the proximity to where we *wanted* to be, but could find no reasonable means of *getting from here to there*.

Eventually, we made an unwise and treacherous climb up the cliff wall, unaided by all the safety equipment we'd learned about. We collapsed and slept at the top of the cliff and were found the following morning. But that palpable sense of not knowing how to get *from here to there* stuck with me.

## LOOKING FORWARD WITH FRUSTRATION

If *here* is exile, and *there* is a life of Hope, where's the onramp? And if it's true that Hope comes as a gift with the presence of God, what are the practices that can open us up and keep us from living out the Hope enemies we've just talked about? I'm convinced—both by experience and Scripture—that the first push on the flywheel of Hope is to name our dissatisfaction, to be honest with ourselves about exactly why exile is less than what we long for.

Yes, sometimes exile is 180 degrees off course—the opposite of what we want. But sometimes exile feels like a parallel highway, within view of the life we long for but decidedly not it.

If we want Hope—real, transformative Hope (not merely optimism)—then we must move to the center of our dissatisfaction. Identifying dissatisfaction is practice number one in opening us up for a transformed, hopeful future.

Sam is a twenty-four-year-old leader in the young adult ministry at my church. He and I are both volunteers in our church's middle school ministry, and I've come to know him as a beautiful young man: warm and friendly, funny and charming, generous with his presence and time, wildly creative, and wonderfully honest.

As a young adult, Sam had just stopped working three part-time jobs when we met for coffee: one as a school detention monitor, one leading after-school programs and one running an aspect of our church's children's ministry. With the school year just ending, Sam only had the part-time church job continuing at the moment. He has moved "seven or eight times" in the last few years, and just moved again. He also told me he's thinking of going back to school through an online program.

Knowing Sam, I see him as a bit of an archetype for so many young adults in our world today. And as I'd hoped, he was wonderfully transparent about his indecision and feelings of being stuck.

I asked Sam to imagine his best self, the one he really hoped to be at forty-five years old, and to tell me about him.

Sam paused and took a deep intake of breath. He shook his head a little, then proceeded, "At forty-five, I want to be more settled into who I am, who I'm created to be. I hope I'm more responsible. Of course, I hope I can pay my bills and don't have a bunch of debt. I want to be figuring out how to do relationships well. Married with kids would be wonderful, but I'm trying to work out if I really desire that or if it's just a cultural thing."

What about a career?

Sam struggled to answer, then said, "That's the big question for me and my friends. It might be that I have a job but find my deeper satisfaction in volunteering. I love mentoring people. I don't know if what I would be satisfied doing has a job description. I'm content, but I want more. More passion in life. More room for experimentation, more room for process, and by that I mean ongoing change and experimentation."

I could hear frustration in Sam's voice and asked him what it was. This time he responded quickly. "Myself. My stuckness. My fear. I think, *God, am I ever going to get to the life you want for me?* It feels like failure. Like I'm trying to claw my way out of a mess I've made. This numbs my sense of God. My sense of God gets shut off. And then, when my sense of God gets turned on I feel guilty. I feel like I'm disappointing God."

Sam has been to Haiti a couple times with groups from my church and was preparing to go again in two weeks' time. With that in mind he said, "I'm extremely dissatisfied with the gap between the joy I see in people in Haiti and the injustices I see there. And I feel like if I was who I was made to be, I could do something about that, or at least have a different perspective. The 'Sam I was created to be' is *totally* capable of impacting these issues."

Sam perked up, and I asked what he was feeling.

Sam's words were profound: "I *love* the person I imagine God created me to be, but feel like the me I am is not giving way to the me I could be."

There's the gap again. Words describing exile. But Sam was doing more than grumbling; and he certainly wasn't acquiescing to exile. Sam was brilliantly putting words to his dissatisfaction, naming it. Sam was pushing on the millstone and positioning himself for the gift of Hope.

## THE AMERICAN DREAM IS A LIE

For centuries, the American dream has promised that if you work hard, you can possess the good life. This dream has morphed, to be sure, in its definition. The shift is located in our collective desire of what we want to possess. Even as recently as thirty or forty years ago, the good life was primarily about property ownership with a generous side helping of relationships. That might be a little snarky, but the image of a poor immigrant dreaming of one day owning a piece of land, or a home, and raising a family while putting in "an honest day's work" was as vivid as a Norman Rockwell painting.

My paternal grandparents lived this dream. Maria and Rudy separately left Germany in their middle teenage years, steaming toward the American dream on a ship. Both headed for Detroit, where each had cousins or siblings who had recently put down roots. Eventually meeting and marrying, they lived the life one can imagine them dreaming of as they had one foot on the gangplank and one foot on the ship leaving Europe.

Rudy spent his life as an electrician for Detroit Edison (now called DTE Energy). They had a simple but comfortable home, raising a family of three children (my father included) in Ann Arbor, Michigan. At retirement age, they did what retirees were supposed to do in those days: moved to Clearwater, Florida, to a massive retirement community where she could fill her days with ceramics classes, and he could fill his with golf.

By twentieth-century standards, they lived the American dream.

But the twenty-first century has a different set of values. Today's American dream is about possessing happiness, not property. Material things are still a major part of the picture (maybe more than ever), since the assumption for many is that "stuff" will provide happiness.

But increasingly, today's young adults (and thirty- and forty- and fifty-somethings) are less interested in property possession and raising a family, and are more interested in a variety of other perceived happiness producers: fun, travel, adventure, meaning or significance, community, and freedom (not freedom to own things, but freedom from being anchored to anything).

The old American dream was easier to realize. While certainly not everyone had the same opportunities to "work hard and make something of themselves" (minorities and women were often not included in this equation), our culture generally provided the means of simple success.

Today's dreamers find it difficult to realize either the old or the new dream. The old is stymied by elevated home prices and an almost-complete elimination of broader support systems (usually provided by extended family). And the new dream is daunting if only due to its lack of clear definition, let alone the extremely elusive nature of reaching the goal.

Dreamers hear stories of people who have the life they want—freedom, adventure, significance—and wait for it to come to them. They usually have no idea how to seek it (if seeking it is even possible). Today's American dream has become the luck of winning the Powerball.

The old American dream was problematic in that it told people they had arrived at the good life (sort of Hope's folksy-but-dim cousin) as soon as they landed at property ownership and a family. It was misleading, but achievable. But the new American dream is a frustration maker, leaving the overwhelming majority completely isolated from the fulfillment they desire. The problem is *not* in longing for freedom, adventure or significance. Those are all lovely things I want also. The problem is in the lie that luck, positivity or grit will get you satisfaction.

And then there's this: most of us aren't sure what we really want, or even what we *should* want. We've been inundated with so many messages about what we *should* want that our deepest longings get obscured beneath layers of propaganda. Apparently (we're told, and we believe) our lives will be perfect, hope filled and satisfying if we have that car, or that sex life, or that body, or that vacation.

How can we begin to name our deepest longings? We start by naming our dissatisfaction: what is it, really, about this exile that is *not good enough*?

## THE STUCKNESS OF TWENTY-SOMETHINGS

This practice of honestly naming our dissatisfaction isn't as easy as it sounds. But there's a group of people who might be helpful in leading us, a group not as far down the path of hope-by-possession. They're a group more naturally in touch with their dissatisfaction since they still carry the developmentally normal passion of youth, but are weary of the exile our culture has thrown them into. That group: twenty-somethings.

A truly strange set of variables have combined over the last decade or two to create an understandable place of frustration and dissatisfaction for today's twenty-somethings. As lies and half-truths often do, it presents itself as a good thing. But it's not.

I was in the middle of a four-hour parent training seminar for a racially diverse group of parents in the Seattle area. I mentioned that adolescence is widely considered to extend, on average, all the way to thirty years old. A parent shouted out from the audience: *I do not receive that!*

Hilarious. But I find that most parents (and older adults) observe this shift taking place in teenagers and young adults, but are quite baffled as to its cause.

Our culture isolates teenagers (and increasingly, young adults), resulting in them spending all their time in a homogeneous group, and they are almost never invited into the world of adults. The only adults most teenagers spend any time with are those adults who come into the world of teenagers (which is good, but not the same thing).

There's been a massive shift in the last ten to fifteen years in treating teenagers (and increasingly, younger twenty-somethings) as if they were children. This is theoretically done in the spirit of "protecting them," but actually does them harm. We don't give them meaningful responsibilities, including in most of our churches, for a bunch of reasons (it's messy when we do, we don't think they're capable). We remove the consequences of their choices in the spirit of "protecting them" or "allowing them to be children."

Bottom line: we can't expect twenty-somethings (or teenagers!) to take responsibility for themselves when they've never been given responsibilities.

Adolescence in America is an archetype of exile. And now it's twenty years long. Everything in our culture tells teenagers and twenty-somethings they are *not yet* adults. They are *other*. They are told they are *not ready*. Then we further isolate them by blaming them for not stepping up and taking responsibility for themselves while in their twenties. It's an all-encompassing, culturally endorsed program of isolation, resulting in deep dissatisfaction.

Adolescence was first described in detail (and the word popularized) by America's first child psychologist, a guy named G. Stanley Hall, in 1904. (I'd love to go off on a long diatribe against Hall, as I believe he did us all a great disservice in so many ways, creating a set of labels and beliefs about adolescents based on a quirky, now completely discredited Victorian evolutionary notion called *recapitulation*. But I'll have to save that for a different book, I suppose.)

Hall, however, established our ways of talking about and understanding adolescence. He used (as we still do) puberty as the starting point of adolescence (certainly there's a cultural starting point, but that has traditionally—or at least until recently—closely paralleled the onset of puberty). And Hall, since he was the first to describe adolescence (at least in modern times), wrote (in essence) that it ends when one is taking responsibility for oneself.

But—here's a wild fact—Hall said, in 1904, that adolescence began at fourteen and a half years old (on average) and ended at about sixteen years old. Eighteen months long. At this point in history, the "holding period" of adolescent exile was more of an elongated transition than a protracted exile.

By the 1970s, with the creation of mandatory secondary education through twelfth grade (in the 1940s and 1950s), and the rise of youth culture (in the 1950s and 1960s) that developed as a result of penning up teenagers in homogeneous classrooms all day long, we came to understand adolescence as that in-between life stage that lasts from thirteen to eighteen years old.

But today, adolescence is considered to start roughly around ten or eleven years old, and last—on average—all the way through the twenties (long enough, by the way, that it's now talked about in three sub-stages: early adolescence from ten or eleven to roughly fourteen; middle adolescence or late teenage, roughly fifteen to twenty; and "emerging adult," the twenty-something years).

When I talk about this stuff to parents and youth workers, people are quick to see the realities in our culture. But they're also quick to point at twenty-somethings and say, "Why won't they just grow up? Why won't they take responsibility for themselves?"

My belief is that this finger is pointing 180 degrees in the wrong direction. We (our culture, our parenting, even our churches) have created this reality of extended adolescence through isolation, through forced exile.

And while twenty-somethings might not show excitement at the prospect of "responsibility" as we have attempted to describe it (remember the shifting American dream, from property ownership to happiness), this limbo-like holding period can often come with a massive subterranean dose of dissatisfaction.

It's the gap again: this time, it's the gap between what I'm told I should want and what I really want. *And* it's the gap between what I want (even if I'm still figuring that out) and seeing any viable means of achieving it.

In many ways, today's twenty-somethings are the most dissatisfied

American generation in our short history. And while others might label them "slackers" because of this, my response is twofold: First, of course they're stuck! We stuck them! And second, good. If twenty-somethings are dissatisfied, then we (people older than "emerging adults") should be looking to them as canaries in the coal mine, alerting us to the potential role of dissatisfaction. Their natural dissatisfaction with the way things are (*your* natural dissatisfaction with the way things are, if you're a twenty-something reader, or really, anyone of any age who feels this way) means they are more easily and naturally in touch with the postures needed for Hope's arrival.

## CHECKING IN WITH ISAIAH

Anyone who wants to understand what the Bible has to say about Hope will eventually need to check in with Isaiah. While the exodus and Moses' seabed adventures gives us a fantastic case study for reflection, Isaiah provides *both* a case study *and* sixty-six chapters of instruction. Really, the pattern and postures for Hope's arrival that this book is built on come mostly, or at least firstly, from the book of Isaiah.

I'm sure there are a small percentage of readers who fully know the story that becomes the backdrop for Isaiah's masterful writing. But my guess is that many of you are more like me: familiar with stuff ("Yeah, I've heard that somewhere"), but not able to quickly pull up a mental map that would guide you through a short discussion of Hope in the book of Isaiah.

So, for readers like me, let's start with a very small portion of history.

Geographically and politically, the Hebrew people were divided into two kingdoms: Israel (which had its capital in Samaria), and Judah, which had its capital in Jerusalem. Isaiah was a prophet in Jerusalem, speaking (and writing) to the people of Judah.

Both kingdoms were minor players in terms of power. The big powerhouses of the day were Egypt (to the south) and Assyria (to the northeast, in modern-day Turkey, Syria, Iraq and Iran). A third superpower was soon to be on the rise, and ended up playing a naming role in what's commonly called the Babylonian Exile. Babylon was also northeast of Judah, just south of Assyria, in modern-day Iraq.

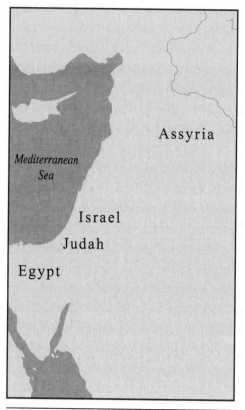

Figure 4.1. Israel and Judah in Isaiah's time

Here's why this geographical understanding matters. Judah was caught in the middle. And since they had little power compared to the superpowers of their day, their options were limited. Isaiah's prophetic ministry started at the tail end of King Uzziah's reign, in the 740s B.C. This is an important framing, because Uzziah's reign was marked as a time of relative prosperity.

Put those factors together—relative prosperity and a lack of power compared to encroaching superpowers from multiple directions—and you end up with a reality that is unfortunately common: assimilation. In Judah, the people of means, including the government, were constantly becoming like the nation(s) they wanted to align themselves with. It was a period of wholesale acquiescence. And while they may have kept an external shell of religion chugging along, their worldviews and values and daily practices—the contents of their hearts—flowed more from their self-serving acceptance of an ideology at odds with their stated faith.

This is the focus of Isaiah's initial prophecy, a blasting at capitulation.

Scholars see the book of Isaiah as two or three sections, so unique in message and tone that they're sometimes referred to as First Isaiah, Second Isaiah and Third Isaiah. Here's the breakdown, with Old Testament scholar Walter Brueggemann's description of the three parts.

In chapters 1–39, which Brueggemann refers to as a "critique of ideology," Isaiah points out the lies of the soup they've been soaking in (much of which led to the prophesied Babylonian exile), their self-deception and their religion that served merely to affirm what they wanted to do.[1]

Chapters 40–55 focus on an "embracing of pain," suggesting that suffering is a *vocation* to be embraced.

Then in chapters 56–66, Isaiah draws out an "unleashing of social imagination," painting a picture of the new, hopeful potential.

Let's unpack the first two a bit, both in their historical setting and the parallels to our own lives (we'll come back to Third Isaiah in chapter eight).

*First Isaiah: pre-exile.* Life in Jerusalem during First Isaiah was marked by a preponderance of looking out for number one. The relative prosperity (certainly not everyone was prosperous, and those who were achieved their wealth, at least in part, by ignoring the needs of others), combined with capitulation to the values, practices and priorities of the various encroaching superpower cultures, led to a state where Hope is impossible. That state: arrogance.

This is no more baldly captured than in the life story of King Uzziah himself. The litany of kings before and after Uzziah, listed in varying detail in 2 Chronicles, reads like an evil amusement park ride of ups and downs. Sixteen different kings are listed: six of them are summarized with some version of "He did what was right in the eyes of the Lord," eight of them have something like "He did evil in the eyes of the Lord" at the top of their résumés and two are given a bit of a "Some evil, some good" synopsis. Chronologically, Uzziah is found right in the middle of the list, which wraps up with the fall of Jerusalem and the beginning of the Babylonian exile.

Reading this list in 2 Chronicles could give you royal whiplash, or at least a bad motion-induced nausea. There are a few blips of righteousness here and there (most notably with Josiah), but there's a whole heap of arrogance and evil.

Back to Uzziah. He started out okay—seeking God. But he got caught up in arrogance, and it was his undoing. Here's 2 Chronicles 26:16-21:

> But after Uzziah became powerful, his pride led to his downfall. He was unfaithful to the LORD his God, and entered the temple of the LORD to burn incense on the altar of incense. Azariah the priest with eighty other courageous priests of the LORD followed him in. They confronted King Uzziah and said, "It is not right for you, Uzziah, to burn incense to the Lord. That is for the priests, the descendants of Aaron, who have been consecrated to burn incense. Leave the sanctuary, for you have been unfaithful; and you will not be honored by the LORD God."
>
> Uzziah, who had a censer in his hand ready to burn incense, became angry. While he was raging at the priests in their presence before the incense altar in the LORD's temple, leprosy broke out on his forehead. When Azariah the chief priest and all the other priests looked at him, they saw that he had leprosy on his forehead, so they hurried him out. Indeed, he himself was eager to leave, because the LORD had afflicted him.
>
> King Uzziah had leprosy until the day he died. He lived in a separate house—leprous, and banned from the temple of the LORD.

I think the line "Indeed, he himself was eager to leave" is one of the more hilariously understated sentences in the Bible.

The implications of Uzziah's leprosy were much greater than "Oh, no, I've got a disease." Not only did leprosy mean he was no longer allowed in the temple, but also that he was relationally cut off.

Uzziah's life is a profound lesson about arrogance. But it's also a picture into the soul of a nation.

If cynicism is the polar opposite of Hope, then arrogance is on another planet. Arrogance keeps us miles and miles away from any possibility of Hope. Arrogance isn't even aware of a need for Hope, since it is—at its core—completely misplaced hope. And of course, arrogance puts a muzzle on naming dissatisfaction, replacing it with the false confidence of attempted control.

It's easy to spot arrogance in other people—strutting, demanding, nose in the air. It's a little tougher to discern it in ourselves. And as someone who has struggled mightily to hand over my arrogance to the painful dismantling of God, I can tell you this: Arrogance is simply the belief that I am capable of saving myself. I am able to meet all my own needs. In short, arrogance says, "I've got this." And with stupidity and blindness, arrogance says this to God.

Let me be 100 percent clear on this. "I've got this" never, ever, ever opens us up to real Hope. How can it, when I'm clearly misplacing all my hope in myself (which, come on, is just so absurd, right?).

Yeah, we've all got a little Uzziah in us. You might be all meek and subservient on the outside, but even you've got some strut hidden away in there somewhere.

**Second Isaiah.** Here's the fascinating bit about Second Isaiah. Isaiah shifts his tone dramatically, and moves into fifteen chapters of sympathetically lamenting the pain of exile—honestly naming, verse after verse, chapter after chapter, the topography of dissatisfaction. The exile hadn't actually come to be, not yet. In reality, it was still roughly a half-century away (the deportations are thought to have occurred in 605, 597, 587/6 and 582 B.C.).

Yet Isaiah speaks clearly, as if from experience, about the lostness of exile, the suffering, the dissatisfaction. In a roundabout way, he helps us to see the *gift* of exile. Exile forces us, very painfully, to break from our arrogance. Exile wakes us up from the lie of "I've got this."

I love this tiny verse from Second Isaiah (40:6): "A voice says, 'Cry out.' And I said, 'What shall I cry?'" At face value, it's a simple interchange between God and Isaiah. But Isaiah's question has a deeper sense to it that connects with our own experiences of exile. Sure, he's asking God for speaking instructions. But he touches on the disorienting "I haven't got this" of waking up in the desert.

And that brutal wake-up call uproots us and places us into a place of potential.

Brueggemann puts it this way:

> Mature personhood does not come by pilgrimages of continuity, but by abrasion, disruption, and discontinuity which shatter our grasp of things and make us, at key points, not the initiators but the recipients of gifts and surprises that we often do not want to receive. . . . The exile is a setting for faith development because it requires relinquishment and abandonment of self in order that the inscrutable power of God may work a genuine newness.[2]

First Isaiah gives us a heads up; but Second Isaiah weeps with us. Second Isaiah helps us name our dissatisfaction. Second Isaiah hints, with a beautiful subtlety, that while "this sucks," there's something better to come.

> So do not fear, for I am with you;
>     do not be dismayed, for I am your God.
> I will strengthen you and help you;
>     I will uphold you with my righteous right hand. (Isaiah
>     41:10)

## EMBRACING DISSATISFACTION IS MOVING TOWARD HOPE

My friend Jon Huckins is involved in peacemaking work in Israel and Palestine. When we were chatting about this book, he shared about a turning point moment for him. He was leading one of his first trips to this war-torn and conflicted area, and found an entirely new perspective in a comment from a peacemaking Jewish man named Shaul. Previously Jon had held, without thinking it through completely, to an undefined sense that peacemaking meant moving away from conflict.

But Shaul said, "If we want peace then we must move to the center of conflict. Conflict creates opportunity for a transformed, hopeful future." A cynic might suggest that change in the Palestinian/Israeli conflict is hopeless, and their best course is to avoid one another. Just as a cynic shies away from risk in order to avoid potential pain, a hopeful seeker of Hope is *willing* to risk. In Shaul's land, honest conversation across Muslim, Jewish and Christian ideologies and convictions is loaded with risk.

A slight variation of Shaul's statement could be made about Hope: *If we want Hope—real, transformative Hope (not merely optimism)— then we must move to the center of dissatisfaction. Dissatisfaction creates opportunity for a transformed, hopeful future.*

Returning to the diagram from chapter two (exile), let's add this first posture, this first practice, of being honest with ourselves about our dissatisfaction:

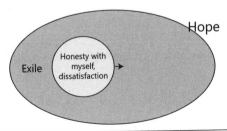

**Figure 4.2**

That's a powerful idea, embracing and naming our dissatisfaction. It's counterintuitive, particularly as a Jesus follower who's been sold the "be happy = be holy" lie.

Here's the way my friend Sam, profiled earlier in this chapter, expressed it: "I have a lot of peers who get dissatisfied and equate that with 'something's wrong with me or others.' They move to blaming. But there's an invitation in this sense of unease—an invitation in that feeling itself—that God is holding something out and waiting for us to step into something new. I've always seen my dissatisfaction as a welcoming thing. 'There's something more for you' is great for inviting Hope!"

## HOPE TOOLBOX

- How does the spiritual practice of naming your dissatisfaction sit with you? Does it make you uncomfortable? Why or why not? How have you experienced pressure to "get over it" or mask it with a happy face?

- If you're serious about positioning yourself for Hope, take time (now, or soon) to get to a quiet place and journal about your dissatisfaction with the way things are. Do this as an unfiltered, stripped-down prayer, believing that God will not be shocked or offended.

- Identify the one or two dissatisfactions that are the most consuming for you, the ones that rob you of life and feel like the worst aspects of exile.

# POSITIONING FOR HOPE

## *Honest Cries to God*

S till in exile, but having been honest with yourself about your longings and deepest dissatisfactions, you've strained and grunted through the first difficult push on the millstone that acts as a flywheel to position yourself for God's gift of Hope. Now it's time for the second push. This one is still tough, and requires you to move your footing and address one of the most difficult issues all humans face: control.

That first push was about honesty with yourself. This second push is about honesty with God, and they're not usually concurrent, and are certainly not the same thing. Only once you've named your dissatisfaction are you able to turn it into a prayer, to offer it up as a cry.

We can't have a conversation about being honest with God without talking about emotions. Think about this: when we stupidly try to *hide* things from God, what is it that we think we're hiding?

I suppose we try to hide our sin. In some sort of theoretically amazing sleight of hand, we think we can presto, abracadabra make God forget that he ever noticed sin in our lives. We foolishly think God likes sparkly objects: church attendance, the occasional act of kindness, dropping ten bucks—*Ten whole dollars, God! Did you SEE that?*—into the offering plate, or in support of that cute coworker's Run For the Cause. I realize this sounds ridiculous; but we totally attempt to pull this off with God. Look God: jazz hands!

The other thing we consistently try to hide from God is our emotions. There are lots of reasons for this:

We have been taught that emotions are bad and can't be trusted. That would mean then that God isn't interested in them.

We're embarrassed by our emotions, and hope that God doesn't actually notice them.

We like to be in control. Expressing emotions (even to God) feels like a lack of control, or—gasp!—a surrendering of control.

We're out of touch with our emotions (I'm looking in the mirror on this one).

But positioning ourselves for Hope, a faithful confidence that God continues to author a story, calls on us to embrace our dissatisfaction, then next nudges us to honestly cry out to God. And we need to express that honest cry to God using a full range of emotions.

## MY SIX-DAY EXPERIMENT IN EMOTIONAL HONESTY

I'd like to model some emotional honesty for you. That sounds absurdly arrogant, as if I have this all figured out and am a paragon of emotional intelligence and honesty. And I'm the most humble man alive!

Really, the absolute truth is that I'm a neophyte when it comes to emotions and emotional honesty. Really, I suck at it. I'm mostly out of touch with my emotions, and I've certainly been known to use manipulation, guilt and other tools as effective means of emotional terrorism.

So I do *not* share as one who has arrived. I share with you as an example of a stooge attempting to be emotionally honest—both with myself and with my God.

After I lost my job and tumbled near the precipice of collapse, I embarked on my own self-imposed desert mini-exile. I was pretty dead, emotionally, by the time I arrived at the layoff. And in the weeks that followed, I went into full-blown emotional freeze. I think this was due to the fact that I was experiencing overwhelming emotions coming at me constantly and from all angles. But I was unable to *experience* them or be honest about them, let alone express them in some form of prayer to God.

I was seeing a therapist for a few weeks, and she suggested that I take five of my days in the desert and give myself, completely, to five emotions. She suggested that I do whatever I needed to do to let each emotion run wild. Air 'em out. Let 'em fly.

Now, not only are we Christians not good at this and we men are often not good at this, I am not good at this. But somehow, the safety and privacy of the desert felt like a place where I wasn't going to anger God. It felt safe enough that I could be honest with myself about what I was feeling. Somehow it felt like a good place to get all Davidic. *Michal, bring me my ephod; I've got some dancing to do.*

Again, I'm not suggesting that my pain is greater than others'. If anything, mine was minor. But it's my story and it's the pain I'm familiar with, the pain within which I took some baby steps of emotional honesty.

Here are a few Davidic Psalms (which I'm including as a reminder that the Bible contains this sort of emotional honesty), and some slightly edited and shortened journal entries from those days.

## ANGER

Appoint someone evil to oppose my enemy;
    let an accuser stand at his right hand.

When he is tried, let him be found guilty,
    and may his prayers condemn him.

May his days be few;
    may another take his place of leadership.

May his children be fatherless
    and his wife a widow.

May his children be wandering beggars;
    may they be driven from their ruined homes.

May a creditor seize all he has;
    may strangers plunder the fruits of his labor.

May no one extend kindness to him

or take pity on his fatherless children.

May his descendants be cut off,
  their names blotted out from the next generation.

May the iniquity of his fathers be remembered before the LORD;
  may the sin of his mother never be blotted out.

May their sins always remain before the LORD,
  that he may blot out their name from the earth. (Psalm
    109:6-15)

My anger bubbles just below the surface. I can feel it there, churning and seething, writhing like a snake being skinned. I can see it, squirming under the parchment of my skin.

I'm afraid of my anger. I don't want it to take control. I'm nervous about allowing it space, or granting it any freedom. If I give it even the smallest bowl of milk, I have this gnawing sense that it will not only stay, but will grow into a feral, feline monster, shredding and screeching and tearing without the goodness to discern.

I want to throw things.

I want to punch and see blood.

But even more than being physical, I want to lash back with words. I want justice, and I want it to hurt (although that's probably not justice, but retribution). I want her to *know* what she's done. I want her to stare that truth in the face. I want her to have to admit it to herself, and weep over her wretchedness, over what she's done, over the unnecessary destruction she has wrought in the name of "what's best for business." I want her to stare blankly into the face of Jesus and see how what she has done *could not* and *does not* align.

My jaw is sore after writing this, as I have been clenching my teeth the whole time. My heartbeat is racing and my muscles are tense. God, grant me justice.

## HURT

You know how I am scorned, disgraced and shamed;
> all my enemies are before you.

Scorn has broken my heart
> and has left me helpless;

I looked for sympathy, but there was none,
> for comforters, but I found none.

They put gall in my food
> and gave me vinegar for my thirst. (Psalm 69:19-21)

> Am I so easily expendable?
>
> Why is "getting me out of the way" the best route?
>
> I think I have given myself to this role in ways you will never live or understand. This wasn't a job for me. This was a calling, and a way to change the world.
>
> I'm only forty-six, and I still feel so young. I feel like I have so much of my life still in front of me. I feel like I was just beginning to really hit my stride in this role, that I was learning humility and how to serve youth workers. I feel like I had a voice and a platform. I did. And it's gone—taken from me for the singular reason of making your budget a little bit better.
>
> God, this hurts so badly. Will I ever heal?

## SADNESS

My God, my God, why have you forsaken me?
> Why are you so far from saving me,
> so far from my cries of anguish?

My God, I cry out by day, but you do not answer,
by night, but I find no rest. (Psalm 22:1-2)

> So much is gone, or at least likely so.
>
> Friendships that won't be maintainable (I see faces as I'm writing this)—people who have meant so much to me, but with whom I won't have natural reason to connect, to intersect our stories, to see each other a couple times a year.
>
> I have a hole the size of the landscape in me. And it's still, and barren, like the desert I'm looking at as I type.
>
> The sun is quickly fading from the sides of the mountains across the desert valley, as it drops behind the ridge behind me. It's only 4:27 p.m. Too early to be evening. Too early for night. That's what this feels like—my daylight has faded, been taken, way too early. Way too capriciously. Way too easily. And it's quiet. And lonely. God, where are you?

## FEAR

Be merciful to me, my God,
for my enemies are in hot pursuit;
all day long they press their attack.

My adversaries pursue me all day long;
in their pride many are attacking me. (Psalm 56:1-2)

> The experience of anxiety has been physical for me in the last few weeks. It's a significant tightening of the muscles in my chest and a shortness of breath (or more like a shallowness of breath—little truncated baby breaths). At the same time, my mind starts to tell stories—negative plausibilities that freight-train into likelihoods. I create fictional reasons for why

this particular thing must be happening, and quickly embrace them as the most probable explanation or outcome. In that space, I'm convinced they're true, or most likely true, even though I can cognitively assent to the possibility that they're not true once the anxiety subsides. But just as often, the tales I tell during those periods become my new reality and I repeat them, cementing them until or unless someone or something intervenes to force a new perspective.

I'm anxious about losing friends, which seems fairly inevitable.

I'm afraid I won't find a meaningful job.

I'm afraid whatever job I find—meaningful or not—will be such a dramatic lowering of income that our family will suffer (which will, as much as I try to convince myself otherwise, totally feel like "my fault").

I'm afraid I'll lose my voice.

I'm afraid I'll lose interest in the things I've been passionate about, especially if I'm in a role that doesn't give me cause to think on them and speak about them.

I'm afraid my kids won't be proud of me and think my job is cool.

I'm afraid the financial stress will bring stress into my relationship with Jeannie, especially since she seems to be way more willing and able to spend less than I do.

I'm afraid I'll have a cool opportunity that will require a move and a boring opportunity that allows us to stay in San Diego, and that I'll have to choose knowing that one seems selfish, and the other feels like death.

I'm afraid of losing our house.

I'm afraid of becoming a shell of myself. I'm afraid that I've "peaked," and nothing else—work-wise—will come close to providing the meaning and fun that I've experienced.

I'm afraid I'll be bored, and even boring.

I'm afraid I'll have to be normal and boring and conventional

> and predictable.
>
> I'm afraid I'll phone it in,
>
> struggle,
>
> have nothing to say,
>
> and no one to say it to.
>
> God, I am overwhelmed with fear and anxiety. I cannot sleep, and I have no rest.

## JOY

Therefore my heart is glad and my tongue rejoices;

my body also will rest secure,

because you will not abandon me to the realm of the dead,

nor will you let your faithful one see decay.

You make known to me the path of life;

you will fill me with joy in your presence,

with eternal pleasures at your right hand. (Psalm 16:9-11)

> (A current-day note: through my four days given to Anger, Hurt, Sadness and Fear, I had the lingering specter of Joy sitting out there laughing at me intimidatingly from then-future day five. But somehow, on the morning of day five, I awoke with a sense of peace—which I'm confident was born out of emotional honesty with God—the first day of joy I had experienced in many months.)
>
> It's interesting to think about all the things I have to be glad about—or, more specifically, all the things that give me joy— particularly at the end of these five days. I feel like the anger has been (to some extent) purged out of me. I'm sure it will still rear its head in the days and weeks to come, but at the moment its fangs are gone.

Last night, after reading a suggestion to make a daily inventory of things I have to be thankful for as I'm laying in bed, I didn't experience any of the nighttime anxiety I've been experiencing so strongly since I've been here. I lay in bed, thinking of my family and friends, and all the good things in my life, and I never once felt afraid. And I slept better than I have the other nights.

When a friend heard I was going out to the desert for these days, he joked that the devil would meet me here and tempt me (a funny little Jesus reference). But there's a sense where it was true: the devils of anger and anxiety and hurt and sadness, the devils of my own projections onto others' motives and projections onto my future, have been very present.

I'm not "all better." I'm not "cleansed." But I do feel like I purged a bit. And this afternoon, as I listened to the sun leak away from the mountains across the valley from where I sit, it doesn't feel like a metaphor for life ending; it feels like peace and quiet and stillness.

Maybe this is a circumstantial hope and peace I'm feeling right now—more a result of the quiet surrounding me and five days of not talking. But at least I've had an appetizer of what I hope and expect to feel in the days to come. At least I've had this dress rehearsal. At least I've been given this gift of foreshadowing.

It's getting darker now—the remaining light of the day is very close to being gone. The single sound I hear other than my keyboard and my breath is the quiet nibbling of a bunny chewing the birdseed I put out earlier. He's looking at me now, between nibbles. Other than that little crunchy sound, there is absolutely no sound at all—no cars, no white noise, no mowers or machinery of any kind. No planes overhead. Nothing. Just the sound of peace. God, give me more peace.

## THE TRUTH ABOUT EMOTIONS

In the past, I would have tried to build a case for emotions by saying, "God invented emotions, so they must be good." But I don't think that's an accurate reflection of the creation story. God is an emotional being, and we are made in the image of God, so we have emotions.

Get this: emotions predate creation.[1]

God didn't "invent" emotions as a component of creation. God invented us and made us with emotions because emotions are a key part of what makes us "made in God's image."

I realize we tend to remake God in our own image. I know I do this—assigning to God my experience in a manner not all that dissimilar from the many times I project my story and experience onto other humans. Any of us are capable of this when we view others as objects rather than persons.

But I don't think I'm projecting my experience on God when I state that God is emotional. I don't think Jesus thought, *Wow, what is this feeling? It's brand new to me!*

In fact, some swing the pendulum the other way and declare that God, who is not bound by humanness, is beyond emotion. But removing emotion from God is merely another approach to remaking God. And that speculative path leaves us with a God who only understands our experience in a conceptual way.

We see God's emotionality throughout Scripture, from the first to last chapter. There's a clear sense of beautiful and deep satisfaction (a feeling!) in God's repeated acknowledgment that each stage of creation was good.

Certainly Jesus experienced emotions in a new, more limited way once he was living as a human.[2] But the emotions themselves weren't new to him. And Scripture clearly tells us Jesus experienced and expressed a full range of emotions. Remember Hebrews 2:17: "For this reason he had to be made like them, fully human in every way."

Fuller Theological Seminary New Testament professor G. Walter Hansen wonderfully summarizes this in a *Christianity Today* article, writing,

The gospel writers paint their portraits of Jesus using a kaleido-scope of brilliant "emotional" colors. Jesus felt *compassion*; he was *angry, indignant*, and *consumed with zeal*; he was *troubled, greatly distressed, very sorrowful, depressed, deeply moved*, and *grieved*; he *sighed*; he *wept* and *sobbed*; he *groaned*; he was in *agony*; he was *surprised* and *amazed*; he *rejoiced* very greatly and was full of *joy*; he greatly *desired*, and he *loved*.[3]

Maybe you have a tiny little itch in your mind at this point, something like, "Yeah, that's Jesus. He was human. But what about God the Father?"

Philip, one of Jesus' disciples, asked a similar question, found in John 14:7-9:

> [Jesus said] "If you really know me, you will know my Father as well. From now on, you do know him and have seen him." Philip said, "Lord, show us the Father and that will be enough for us." Jesus answered: "Don't you know me, Philip, even after I have been among you such a long time? Anyone who has seen me has seen the Father. How can you say, 'Show us the Father'?"

And what about the Holy Spirit?[4]

> In the same way, the Spirit helps us in our weakness. We do not know what we ought to pray for, but the Spirit himself inter-cedes for us through wordless groans. (Romans 8:26)

> And do not grieve the Holy Spirit of God. (Ephesians 4:30)

Now you may have another potentially itchy semiformed thought: *But emotions can be so destructive! Clearly, emotions and sin have some connection.*

The scriptural caution to us is *not* about having emotions, but about what we *do* with them. We've wrongly interpreted Paul's words "Be ye angry, and sin not" to mean that the only valid anger is this thing we've made up called "righteous anger." Whatever. Be angry and express that anger—*especially* to God; don't stuff it or bury it. Just be watchful of the actions that flow out of anger (or hurt, or sadness, or fear). Honestly, some of our emotions are so strong that *only* God can be trusted with them, and God can be trusted with them for any length of time.

Bottom line: our emotions are a massive gift from God and learning to be present to them is part of our created design. So why am I making such a big deal about emotions in this chapter about honest cries to God? Because we only effectively position ourselves for Hope when we practice unadorned, emotional honesty with God. You can try to construct a powerful rhetoric of your laments to God without emotion; but it will be partially or mostly untrue. When we hold back we are, in essence, not being fully honest with God. I'm not suggesting that God is holding back, waiting to see if you'll be honest; what I'm saying is that we will *miss* the presence of God (and the arrival of Hope) if we're still holding on to control, including the controlling of our emotions.

## SPIRITUAL BLOOM AND EMOTIONS

I've noticed something internal over the last few years, something at times strange and at other times beautiful. It has felt like a spiritual softening, or a spiritual awakening. The best words I can come up with to describe it are: I think Jesus has been slow-brewing a mini-revival in me.

It's not that I'd lost my faith. Not at all. But I do think I'd spent many years intellectualizing my faith. And in more recent years, I've been *feeling* my faith.

Maybe it was the pace of the last decade (and, particularly, the soul-deadening exile period I've already written so much about). I certainly believe, and have often publicly said, that busyness is the archenemy of intimacy with God. But even though I've taken multiple silent retreats over the last ten years, there hasn't been much emotional connection to what I believe to be true.

Here's what I'm sensing: I've been re-finding God (or God has been re-finding me) in experience. I need an experience of God to sustain, and possibly grow, my faith. I need an experience of God to know Hope.

Knowing about God is good, understanding things about Scripture is helpful. But I don't experience God in knowledge and understanding. I experience God in worship, in serving, when I'm utilizing my gifts with awareness that they're gifts. When I feel.

Some of this shift is likely due to the emotional work I've done over the past four years. I've stopped dishonoring my emotions (or, at least, I dishonor them less frequently).

But the truly new discovery in my own spiritual journey isn't just that I'm feeling, but that I keep sensing—over and over again—God's presence in the midst of those emotions.

And here's where it goes way beyond psychology and emotions: all of these moments of experiencing God are growing my faith. I actually believe more. In those moments, and more and more often in-between those moments, I am aware of God's realness, and of the loving gaze of Jesus, and of the beauty of the story that God continues to author—in me and through me, and in all of creation. This "more faith" thing infiltrates various arenas of my life, and I find myself meditating concurrent with whatever I'm busy doing. I find myself seeing God in others more. I find myself fueled in the work I have before me.

There's an insecure part of me that is afraid of even naming this, like it's a butterfly that I'll never quite be able to hold on to, even though I'm enjoying its beauty for a few passing minutes. I'll tell you what it feels like: it feels like Hope.

## CONTROL AS CLENCHED HANDS

A few years ago, I came across an old book by the always brilliant and insightful Henri Nouwen, called *With Open Hands*.[5] It's a funky and very dated book about prayer. In it, Nouwen unpacks a simple suggestion that at its core prayer is about releasing control, and he uses the metaphor of opening our clenched and grasping hands.

I've found such deep connection with that idea, with that motion. And while I love Nouwen's focus on prayer, I've found that my absurd obsession with trying to control God is broader than prayer.

Externally, most people wouldn't consider me a "control freak." But who cares if there are people further along the control continuum than I am. The reality is, I must either love control or think it will provide me with something else I desire. And my experience of leading two hundred church leaders through a yearlong intensive coaching program in the past few years has revealed something to me: we're all control freaks.

Here's my working definition of control: *minimizing variables and maximizing efficiencies for predictable outcomes.*

Sounds logical, right? Like, what's wrong with that?

A few months ago I was struggling—obsessing, really—with my income. Being self-employed can have that impact. In my five years of self-employment, I've yet to have a significant financial problem, but that doesn't keep me from freaking out from time to time. I look at my little tracking spreadsheet, and my mind starts to wander down completely useless and unhelpful pathways.

*I'm not going to have enough money.*
*How will I pay my daughter's college fees?*
*What if this is the beginning of the end?*
*We're going to be living in the gutter soon!*

But here I am a few months later, realizing that God provided yet again. It wasn't one of those dramatic stories I've often heard of an anonymous envelope of cash in the mailbox. Instead, it was through the most regular and mundane of provisions: some projects I'd been working on came together.

And I was reminded of a connection that I've learned many times:

the connection between Hope and release. Remember, Hope isn't something we can create. I can't bear down and try harder and suddenly have more Hope.

Instead, Hope is a gift from God. Hope comes to me, usually in the midst of suffering or dissatisfaction with the way things are, and an honest cry out to God.

When I talk to teenagers about the fruit of the Spirit, I try to make a similar point. We don't choose to be fruity. Fruit is a result of a life connected to the Spirit. It's a gift, really.

All the effort in the world, even with the correct leverage, won't suddenly result in love, joy, peace, patience, kindness, goodness, faithfulness, gentleness and self-control.

There's so much I try to control. Finances, Hope, and spiritual fruit are only three of a very, very long list. And I think I'm learning that my open hands toward God—a position of release and request—is the stance that ultimately positions me for what I truly desire.

So then: what role do I play? I mean, I'm supposed to do something, right? Whether in my own interior life or my family's well-being or my desire to experience life-giving Hope: I'm not just supposed to sit and wait, believing that God will do something, right?

That's the tension. Part of me believes that a little more sitting and waiting on God is exactly what's called for, and just might be the antidote to our ongoing forays into control and manipulation.

But I also believe that God invites me to play an active role. I get to participate! I need to be reminded that my active participation with God looks like me being the kid with the weird lunch at the miraculous feeding of the five thousand.

Could Jesus have fed the crowd without the kid's participation? Sure.

Was the kid necessary for the will of God to happen that day? Not really.

Would the miracle have happened were it not for the kid's involvement? We don't know. But we can be confident about this: that kid would never have been the same. You know he told that story to his grandkids.

My personal finances. The fruit of the Spirit in my life. The Hope in my heart. They all beckon with the same invitation: step up, open up your hands, release control and give your "lunch."[6]

Admittedly, I'm an optimist at heart. As a result, I experience a lightening of burden and openness to Hope when I'm honest about my emotions. But I think the same movement holds true for those who are "half-empty glass" people. This is what's so helpful about King David's story and his psalms: he's free and open in both ecstasy and despair.

Hope comes to us when we're honest with God. Hope shows up as we cry out to God with unfiltered emotionality, dropping any pretense that we can control God (or our lives, for that matter) with a restraint of our emotions.

When authors tell me to stop reading and try something, I'm a resister. But I'd love you to try this tiny little exercise: clench your fists. Make them as tight and tense as you can muster. Pay attention to the feelings in the muscles of your hands, arms and shoulders. Hold your hands clenched for a bit. Then . . . slowly open them up, completely letting go of any muscle flexing or intensity. Notice the sensations that come with release and store the memory of that feeling away as a tangible action step in your desire to experience Hope.

Be encouraged that while you still might not feel all that hopeful, you are actively positioning yourself for the arrival of Hope that comes with the presence of God. That movement, those practices, could be visualized like this:

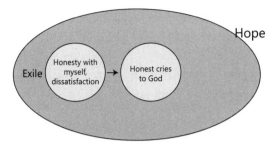

**Figure 5.1**

Naming your dissatisfaction with the way things are and honestly holding out your dissatisfaction, on open hands of emotional cries to God, are quite possibly the only things we can "do" to receive Hope.

## POST-ZOMBIE SOUL

The 2013 zombie film *Warm Bodies* was extremely unique for this weird film genre: it's a zombie love story. I remember watching it on a trans-Pacific flight in the middle of the night, having not heard of it before finding it on my seat-back on-demand video screen. And I remember being very pleasantly surprised.

The film's tagline summarizes the plot, in a sense: *He's still dead, but he's getting warmer.* Basically, it's the story of a zombie guy whose heart gets a super tiny jump-start when he sees a live (non-zombie) young woman. He ends up saving her, and they're forced to spend a bunch of time together in his proto-hipster bachelor pad while the zombie hordes move on by. But, of course, she begins to see the flickers of life in him just as he starts to *feel* them in himself. And love ensues! Yay!

What I found particularly unique about this zombie movie is that it was not about gore or horror or creative sound and visual effects (which are called for, I suppose, when the script calls for the eating of humans). At its heart (ha!), *Warm Bodies* is a film about feeling. Its not-so-subtle message is "to be dead is to feel nothing; even those who no longer feel anything can come back to life, to feeling." There's also a subtle message, an exploration of the soulless zombies that only commodify others for consumption, and how some of the non-zombies in the film fit that description just as easily. Hopeless people are hollow people, zombie or not, and they use others to stave off their emptiness.

In my own mini-exile, I came face to face with the fact that I had developed a zombie soul. In order to press through a horrendous season of life, I had shut down my feelings. And while the soul and feelings are not synonymous, I'm not sure it's possible to have a vibrant soul without authentic feelings. They're symbiotic prerequisites of one another.

Lots of people, I've found, live with a zombie soul. They're going through the movements of life. They may even be going through the movements of a spiritual life. But there's no blood pumping. And there is—by choice or external force—a complete shutting down of honest feelings.

In my own little way, I lived the story of R, the zombie in *Warm Bodies*. The rekindling of my soul was a love interest, just like his. But it wasn't a girl. My love interest—the gentle and present heart sparker of my story—was none other than the Creator of my heart.

A year after that mini-exile in the desert, I wrote this, just after attending and speaking at a large event hosted by the organization I had previously led:

It's Tuesday, October 12, as I write. 8:15 a.m. I woke up this morning in Canebrake Canyon, in the desert east of San Diego. I'm back at the desert home I have retreated to a few times in the past for days of silence. But this is the first time I've been here in a year.

Really, while I'm sure some of this is my personality make-up, I am still—a year later—a bit surprised by how quickly I was lifted out of the overwhelming anxiety of what happened and fear of what was to come, how quickly God pointed me in a new direction, how quickly my heart is healing.

There are still some wounds in there, I'm sure. I really don't think I've stuffed them or buried them; I just think they're the natural sensitive places left over from injury (very much like the sensitivity of the scar on my thumb that's been there since eleventh grade, in 1979). This residual sensitivity was made very clear to me a week and a half ago at an event hosted by the organization I used to lead (an event at which I was to present a couple seminars).

The week before the event, I started to feel something I hadn't felt in a very long time: anxiety. In fact, I was more interested in the foreignness of the feeling than I was in the feeling itself.

I lived with high anxiety (thanks, Mel Brooks) for my last two years at that organization. It was constant. It ruined my sleep, lowered my productivity, and pushed my faith into numbness. My soul was a zombie soul.

So when I felt that anxiety again, for the first time since I left this canyon a year ago, it was more intriguing and encouraging than it was debilitating. I was intrigued by the realization that I hadn't felt that same level of anxiety this past year, even once. And I was encouraged that my life these days is so full of wonderful things and that none of them cause me anxiety (concern and stress from time to time, sure, but not full-on anxiety).

All that said, things were really uncomfortable for me the first day at the event. Even driving into the parking lot of the convention center was awkward. And as I walked from my car to the room where I would check in as a speaker—passing lots of attendees and a handful of people I know—I was seriously battling the impulse to give in to emotional freeze (the gateway to zombie soul). I was twitchy and distracted. I called an old friend by the wrong name. And I was totally living into that classic middle school reality of the imaginary audience: I felt like everyone was glancing my way and wondering (at best) how I was doing or (at worst) how I had the guts to be there after I had (my absurd projection of their thoughts) screwed this company up so deeply.

Eventually, I stood in the back of the opening main session, finding a little relational mooring point first with my church's middle school pastor, and later, with one of my closest friends and former coworkers. They helped normalize the whole thing for me, completely understanding how weird it was for me.

After thirty minutes, though, I realized I had a greater desire to go home and see my wife (due to her travel and mine, I'd literally seen her for fifteen minutes total in the past fourteen days). So I went home. On my way home, I made the decision to give myself permission to lay low for the weekend—to engage or be scarce to whatever level I wanted, without guilt or shoulds. And, over the weekend, things really did shift for me. Engaging youth workers during my seminars was certainly key to this—sensing that I was "in the zone" and had a place at the event.

So, here I am in the desert. It's about a month and a half away from the anniversary of when I came out here last. But today is only a week away from the one-year anniversary of my lay off. Make no mistake: I hope I have learned a great lesson about how not to treat an employee who needs to (for whatever reason) be let go. But my collection of descriptors, as I look back on this past year and take stock of my current reality, are: gratefulness, peace (wow, I really didn't think that would be possible), growing confidence, greater spiritual intimacy and emotional health. And . . . the zombie soul is no more. In its place is a fully alive, warm-to-the-touch, responsive, tender soul. There's surely still some fragility there. But I'll take a fragile living soul over a tough dead one any day.

Reading that entry today, almost five years later (and with close to zero fragility lingering at this point), I feel nothing but thankfulness for my revived soul. And I can see—though I can't take credit for it, since it hardly felt like a conscious choice of my own—that my honesty opened me up to the very present Hope God was bringing.

## Hope Toolbox

- Of the five emotions I wrestled with in the desert—anger, hurt, sadness, fear and joy—which of them is strongest for you when you think about your primary dissatisfactions? Take a moment to *experience* that feeling (even if it seems risky).

- If you didn't do the little clenching your fists and releasing exercise you just read about, try it now. Be sure to pay close attention to the sensations in your body. Consider the ways in which you try to control God, and others, and yourself, and the world around you.

- Clench your hands again. Use your imagination to picture the emotion surrounding your dissatisfaction being tightly ensconced in your fists. Then, as a courageous and prayerful act of faith, open up your hands and offer that feeling to God.

# SIX

# THE PUSHBACK

*Fear*

I almost died in a snowdrift in Alaska when I was thirteen. At least I thought I was going to die, and in hindsight it sure seems like a close call.

My dad was a fundraising guy for a mission organization. And after he completed funding for a small airplane to serve the remote areas of their work in Alaska, I flew with him and a couple others when the plane was delivered from our home in the Detroit area. It was a little six-seat Cessna, and it took portions of three days to get us there.

We were in Alaska for a couple weeks, much of it in the small town of Glenallen, a tiny town (population 483!) that was the mission's headquarters in Alaska, the then-home of Alaska Bible College, and a temporarily booming economy thanks to the Trans-Alaskan Pipeline. Since my dad was in meetings most of the time, and the local kids were in school, I had quite a bit of time to myself. But it was January, and the temperatures were hitting record lows (think -20 to -50 degrees Fahrenheit).

My salvation from boredom came in the form of a snowmobile. A friendly missionary kid my own age, Nate, let me borrow it while he was in school. And the fact that I was allowed to ride off into the surrounding wilderness all by myself, all day long, says something about shifts in parenting styles from the 1970s to today.

For a couple days I was extremely cautious, never going very far or fast. I gingerly wove my way down clear trails through forests and timidly accelerated a bit more across frozen lakes. But as the days went by, I did exactly what you would expect a seventh grade boy to do: I got stupid.

It was the middle of the afternoon and the sun was out, which made the temperature, when I was fully bundled up, nominally tolerable. And I'd been riding for an hour or so, feeling like a pro in the way I could now handle the beast. I remember clearly that I was riding down a wide path—probably a two-track dirt road during summer. And I wasn't watching where I was going. All I can remember is a sudden flurry of snow and tumbling and the snowmobile disappearing and me coming to a stop completely encased in very loose snow.

Apparently, there was a large pit of some sort right in the middle of the path I was barreling down, and it was at least partially covered in snow. I can't remember the size of it, or even the physics of why I couldn't get out. But I sure do remember the panic of *trying* to climb out of that snowy pit and not succeeding. I ratcheted multiple times through a list of three actions:

Screaming for help.

Kicking and clawing and scrambling in a desperate attempt to get free.

Stopping to catch my breath and allowing an overwhelming sense of fear to overtake me.

I really have absolutely no idea how long I was in the snowy pit. It felt like hours, and I'm sure it wasn't mere minutes. The cold started to creep in and I stopped trying to escape. I was embarrassed and mad and miserable and completely terrified. It became clear to me that I was going to die, buried alive in this white grave. Sure, I reasoned, they would find me eventually, but it would be too late.

Except for good ol' Nate. He had a daily after-school routine of snowshoeing to all his animal traps. And I just happened to be on his route that day.

## WHY FEAR? WHY NOW?

Think of a time when you were gripped with fear. What was the feeling *behind* the fear?

When I was facing my icy death in that snowy pit, the "presenting" issue was a fear of death, I suppose. But the deeper issue, the root cause, was my overwhelming sense of helplessness. It had become increasingly clear to me that there was nothing I could do to save myself.

I've read about, and seen in movies, people who—facing imminent and inevitable death—move beyond fear to a place of calm. Of course plenty of Christian saints, modern and ancient, known and unknown, slip from life without fear, with a confidence (a Hope) about what's next. But whether it was spiritual immaturity or just plain old immaturity (I was thirteen!), I wasn't there. At least not by the time Nate showed up.

Maybe I can go a step further: my feeling of helplessness was a sense of exposure (both literally and otherwise). And that idea—exposure—just might be the prime answer for why we experience fear.

There are two kinds of people who don't struggle as often with fear: those who have found a deep and unwavering sense of Hope, and those who are still living in arrogant denial, believing that "I've got this."

That means there are three kinds of people in the world:

Those who truly believe they are in control, and therefore don't experience fear.

Those who have received the gift of Hope that comes like the breath of God, and therefore don't have fear.

All of those messy people in the middle who may or may not show it, but are riddled with fear.

I've been all three of these at various points in my life. Heck, I think I've been all three of these at various points today!

So why is there a chapter on fear in a book about Hope? And hasn't fear been a part of the equation the whole time, profoundly marking us while in exile, interlaced with our attempts at honesty with self and God? Of course! Fear is not *new* to us after naming our dissatisfaction and honestly crying out to God. But my experience, and what I've seen in others and the stories of Scripture, is that fear comes at us like a freight train in the liminal space after we unclench our fists and release control.

We're not making Hope happen. We're attempting to position ourselves—open ourselves up—to the possibility of Hope arriving with the presence of Jesus. We try to control things *because* of our fears; but releasing control unmasks us and leaves us vulnerable.

Think of it this way: a wild animal (say, a feral dog) instinctively knows to protect its neck. The neck is the most vulnerable spot on most mammals. That's why a wild dog keeps his head down as he cautiously approaches you. And you know that an animal feels absolutely and completely safe when it is willing to stretch out and expose its neck. This is a signal that the animal trusts. But make a sudden movement, and that neck will be instantly protected once again.

We do the same thing. We grip tightly, attempting to control our pain and our experience of the world around us. But when we posture ourselves honestly before God, releasing control, we are exposed. Vulnerable. Helpless. Waiting.

And in that vulnerable place of exposure, waiting for the presence of God and Hope's arrival, our fears about ourselves and God often sound off like trumpet blasts, urging us to clench again, to regain control, to step back from the blinding light of exposure.

Fear is a semipermeable wall in our movement toward receiving Hope.

*What if there really isn't anything better than this?*

*What if I deserve this?*

*What if God doesn't exist? Or doesn't hear me? Or doesn't care? Or is unable to do anything to help?*

*What if God provides a solution that is worse than my previous dissatisfaction?*

There's no way around this: it's a horribly scary place. Exposed and naked, buffeted by gale-force winds of doubt and shame and uncertainty. Many people, maybe most, collapse and retreat. Grasping and clenching for control once again, high-tailing it back to Egypt, back to the *known* of exile.

Here's where the semipermeable wall of fear falls in our unfolding diagram of Hope:

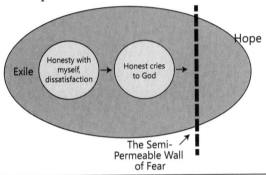

**Figure 6.1**

## BACK TO MY DESERT

When I arrived at my self-imposed mini-exile in the desert after losing my job (and *feeling* that I had lost so much more than employment—that I'd lost my future), I was completely overcome with fear. The other emotions I wrote about (anger, hurt, sadness) were all secondary to the incapacitating barrage of fear.

By the time I arrived in the desert, my fears wouldn't be chained in the basement of my soul and psyche. They'd broken free, and wanted to destroy me.

But I named my fears. Pages and pages of naming, actually. I stared them in the face and looked into their evil yellow eyes. And something unexpected happened: they cowered, just a bit. Instead of *me* being exposed, *they* were suddenly exposed.

That was roughly five years ago. And—this is going to sound strange, so stick with me—I now think of those fears almost like friends, albeit dysfunctional friends that can seriously jack with my life.

Listen: *my fears have not gone away.* They seem almost like a cross to carry. They're part of me, like a pet that could scratch my eyes out but mostly lies innocuously in the corner. Naming them starts to defang them and begins the process of disempowering them.

And by being aware of my fears, I'm able to consciously and consistently hold them up in the palms of my hands, as a prayer to Jesus, the one who longs to bring me Hope. I'm not completely sure why Jesus doesn't totally remove them from me (probably something about keeping me humble, or living into a life of faith); but I'm okay with that.

## WHAT ARE WE AFRAID OF?

So what are all these fears I'm referring to? My fear of death by freezing in the Alaskan pit seems pretty black and white. Your fear during a time of exile might be easy to identify. But most of our fears, especially in that space of open vulnerability after releasing control, are much more slippery and difficult to identify. We usually have years of experience at masking them and mislabeling them and hiding them in deep internal wells.

*Fears about ourselves.* Certainly, when we stand in that exposed and naked place of honesty with ourselves and God, some of our fears are about ourselves.

*I'll be exposed for who I really am.* It's one thing to be honest with myself and God, but it's a whole different enchilada to be honest with all the people in my life. When we open our hands and release control, we often feel dangerously exposed. It's one thing to stand in my bathroom with no clothes on, with no one to see me but God and my own eyes in the mirror; but standing naked on a street corner is something only weirdoes do, right?

The fear of exposure is a fear of being found out for who I really am.

The job loss I have written about so much in this book was actually my second job loss. My first was an actual firing (not a botched layoff). I was a young junior high pastor, having a blast leading a healthy and growing ministry. Every single indication and measurement should have said that things were going extremely well. But I'd naively gotten sideways with a couple powerful elders in the church—the church board chairman and the treasurer. They had attempted to bend me to their agendas (which they did with everyone, and with the entire church), and I was immature and inexperienced enough with that sort of manipulation to not notice most of it, and blissfully dismiss the bits I did notice.

Three years in, a relatively tiny incident occurred where I mishandled a small accounting issue: no malice or evil intent on my part, just rookie naiveté and sloppiness. But that became both the tipping point and a rationale for something of a trial. When the actual facts didn't seem like enough to warrant their disapproval of me, they converted all their pent-up (and misplaced) mistrust of me into character accusations: *You are a liar. You are a manipulator. You are insubordinate. You are untrustworthy. You are a poor role model. There's nothing you can do to change how we feel about you, so you need to leave. Today. But we love you, and want to take care of you, so we'll give you two weeks' pay.* (I'm not making that up. That's literally what they said.)

The weeks and months following that experience were filled with fear. In that case, the fear was all anchored in exposure. I was pretty sure the character accusations weren't true; but I was plagued with an overwhelming self-doubt that: (a) maybe they're right, and (b) what if everyone else finds this out about me?

*I'll lose something I care about, or something that gives me a sense of control.* Living in denial of our dissatisfaction allows us to hold on to what is, or at least what we perceive to be, reality. If I don't acknowledge and express my longings to myself and to God, it's not a stretch to convince myself that I can continue to control at least what I've currently been controlling. Sure, it might be far less than perfectly satisfying; but it's *something* rather than *nothing*.

A big part of my fear in the desert was superglued to potential loss. I assumed I was not only losing a job, but also losing myself. It wasn't merely the loss of security, it was the loss of the image I had so carefully and painstakingly crafted.

This fear is patently obvious in the story of the Israelites Moses led through the Red Sea. When they grew fearful in the desert and cried out, "It would have been better for us to serve the Egyptians than to die in the desert!" (Exodus 14:12), they were expressing their fear of loss.

*This is all there is.* Moving through the postures we've talked about, and standing in that space between an honest cry out to God and the wall of fear, can easily lead one to a bit of an existential crisis. This isn't the fear that God doesn't exist (we'll get to that in a second); instead, this fear is nihilism: *What if life has no meaning, no purpose, no value?*

This fear often masquerades as cynicism. Cynicism isn't always the cavalier hipster aloofness we see in two-dimensional media portrayals, celebrity caricatures and social media profiles. The fear that the exile I'm hoping to leave is all there is gets verbalized as "Nothing ever changes," and "I'm fooling myself to think there's more to life than this pain."

This quiet and barren place alongside the wall of fear is lonely.

**Fears about God.** The fears about ourselves are common and vicious. But since this intentional posturing for Hope is an inherently spiritual expedition, the fears that blast, coax and seduce, or wither us back to exile are more often fears about God.

In my youth pastor coaching groups we talk about the voices of resistance that keep us from experiencing God's best for us. I spend some time talking about the voice of judgment ("Change isn't necessary"), the voice of cynicism ("Change isn't possible") and the voice

of fear ("If change happens, I'll lose something"). Then I have participants spend time in reflection, considering which voice of resistance is most common to their own struggle with not experiencing
the presence of God. Participants return to the group and share what
they've discovered. And while the two other voices (judgment and
cynicism), as well as fears about ourselves, are occasionally expressed,
fears about God are the most common (at least for those who are able
to be truly honest).

What are those fears about God that encourage us to re-grip
control in our place of exposure?

*God is unaware.* If you've been around the block with church and
Christianity and the Bible, as I have, you can spout the rational propo-
sitions for the omniscience of God. God is all-knowing. There's nothing
that happens anywhere in all of creation that God isn't aware of.

Yet, it sure doesn't always feel that way. In fact, my own pain can
sometimes leave me with a sense that I only have three non-
overlapping, completely exclusive options to choose from:

God doesn't really see me standing here exposed and raw and
crying out for help.

God sees, maybe something, but is dispassionate.

Or, I'll stuff what I'm actually feeling, take some Lithium, and
pretend my unease just needs to be shaken off like a moment of
déjà vu.

Of course, none of those options gets me past the fear, past the wall.

This fear is expressed all over the place in the Bible, often by men
and women we consider champions of faith. When the disciples were
out in a boat and caught off-guard by a major storm, the boat almost
scuttled. Jesus, apparently, did not struggle with seasickness:

> Jesus was in the stern, sleeping on a cushion. The disciples woke
> him and said to him, "Teacher, don't you care if we drown?"
> (Mark 4:38)

Their question was a pointed way of asking, "Are you *even aware* of the predicament we're in here?"

King David expresses this fear over and over again in the Psalms. One of many examples is found in Psalm 10:1:

> Why, LORD, do you stand far off?
> Why do you hide yourself in times of trouble?

Clearly, you are not alone if you sense this fear. A great many saints have gone before you on this one. So it's normal, and shouldn't be cause for shaming yourself. But that doesn't mean it's helpful.[1]

*God doesn't care.* I have a friend who had one of the most horrific childhoods I have ever heard of. Among a plethora of other atrocities, her staunchly religious father repeatedly raped her from childhood throughout her teenage years. He would even say the Lord's Prayer or quote Scripture *while* raping her.[2]

As you can imagine, this friend struggled to find an understanding of God that would frame, or would even have permitted, her experience. In our many conversations about faith (she desperately wanted to hold on to faith amidst all her doubts), she regularly articulated, quite understandably, some form of "If God *can* intervene, then why didn't he? Clearly, he didn't care enough to somehow stop my father from raping me."

Your experience doesn't have to be as patently criminal and from the deepest pit of hell as my friend's for you to be confronted with this fear. After all, we've all experienced asking for help only to discover that the person we asked didn't care enough to respond. And, we've all *been* the person who didn't care enough to respond when someone asked for help. So we project our human brokenness onto God while in that liminal, nether region alongside the Wall of Fear.

The shadow side of this fear comes from our own wounded self-images: "I'm not worthy of God's care," or "I'm not significant enough to warrant God's care." Some form of these statements, usually masked in layers of slightly less self-deprecating language, is the single most common fear I hear from church leaders in my coaching groups.

*God isn't able to do anything.* If I believe that God sees and hears my cries and really does care, but the solution or rescue or peace or Hope doesn't immediately show up, it's not a big leap of imagination to suspect that God is simply not powerful enough to make a difference.

Again, many of us can rattle off the things we've been taught about God's omnipotence. God is all-powerful. There's nothing God can't do other than go against God's own character.

But in that open-handed waiting place of exposure, the evil one whispers to us. And his voice sounds like our own thoughts: *Maybe God isn't who I thought God was.*

Honestly, this is probably the easiest (and therefore, one of the most common) ways of dealing with the problem of evil. If you still have faith that God exists, and choose to believe that God cares, then the simplest way to explain the Holocaust and the Rwandan genocide and tsunamis and earthquakes that destroy countless lives is to have sympathy on a God who just can't quite bring the intervention.

I'm deeply saddened by the number of my friends whose faith has been undone by an acceptance of this logic as a means to rationalize their fears.

*God will provide in a way I don't want.* Ah, this fear is a killer, and so prevalent. It's built on a flawed theology, but that cognitive acknowledgment isn't very helpful when this fear pours down on you, since it's a *feeling* rooted in belief formed over time. I find it's not uncommon at all for those raised in a particularly conservative or borderline legalistic faith culture.

When we were working through the voices of resistance with one of my coaching groups, one of the guys struggled to articulate his fear. Trevor sashayed around the issue, struggling to reconcile what he *knew*, theologically, with what he *experienced* in real life. He was a guy much like Alex, whose story I shared in the introduction, who couldn't quite figure out how to get onto the fast lane toward the life he wanted. But in this case, Trevor's fear was centered on what he perceived to be a potential rub between what he wanted in life and what God wanted for him. He kept talking about God's will, but when he used that term, he was clearly implying something that wouldn't make him happy.

I finally asked him, bluntly, if he was trying to say that his fear is that God's will would be something bad for him?

"No, of course not," he responded. "Surely God's will for my life would be the best thing."

Then some variation of that?

He stammered, then finally admitted, "I guess I just think . . . it seems like . . . God's will . . . yeah, I think, or fear, that God might have plans for me that won't really be something I would ever actually want or enjoy, and that it'll feel more like duty than life."

Ugh. That's a painful and debilitating place to be. Trevor might as well have said, "God doesn't really *like* me; I'm merely a tool in God's cosmic plan." That might get you your self-denial badge, but it's not much of a welcome mat for Hope. Hello, exile, good to see you again!

## FEARING THE PROMISED LAND

Remember the Israelites, wandering around the desert after God's miraculous rescue in the exodus? Are you familiar with the part of their story when they first approached the Promised Land, the land "flowing with milk and honey" that Moses had told them about? They too had gone from exile to plenty of honesty about their dissatisfaction, to buckets of honest, open-handed cries to God. They were exposed and waiting for an influx of Hope, a realization of their collective dreams, when they ran headfirst into the wall of fear.

When they approached the Promised Land (Canaan), Moses gave them God's instructions, that they should send one man from each of the twelve tribes to explore the land and report back:

> Go up through the Negev and on into the hill country. See what the land is like and whether the people who live there are strong or weak, few or many. What kind of land do they live in? Is it good or bad? What kind of towns do they live in? Are they unwalled or fortified? How is the soil? Is it fertile or poor? Are there trees in it or not? Do your best to bring back some of the fruit of the land. (Numbers 13:17-20)

The band of merry men did as they were instructed, and were gone for forty days. Their report reads like a laundry list of fear:

> We went into the land to which you sent us, and it does flow with milk and honey! Here is its fruit. But the people who live there are powerful, and the cities are fortified and very large. (Numbers 13:27-28)

But Caleb and Joshua, two of the twelve, didn't agree. If they had any fear, they must have been able to name it and lay it aside. Caleb jumped in with a hopeful alternate perspective:

> We should go up and take possession of the land, for we can certainly do it. (Numbers 13:30)

However, the voices of fear were loud.

> But the men who had gone up with him said, "We can't attack those people; they are stronger than we are." And they spread among the Israelites a bad report about the land they had explored. They said, "The land we explored devours those living in it. All the people we saw there are of great size. We saw the Nephilim there (the descendants of Anak come from the Nephilim). We seemed like grasshoppers in our own eyes, and we looked the same to them." (Numbers 13:31-33)

It's probably not fair to assume I know the exact nature of their fear. But it sure reads like:

*We'll experience loss.*
*God isn't powerful enough for this.*
*God's solution for us is bad!*

The fear of the ten ignited like wildfire among the people, and they begged to return to the horrible-but-known place of exile:

> If only we had died in Egypt! Or in this wilderness! Why is the LORD bringing us to this land only to let us fall by the sword? Our wives and children will be taken as plunder. Wouldn't it be better for us to go back to Egypt? (Numbers 14:2-3)

As much as we'd like to scoff at the Israelites' lack of faith in the face of fear, we'd need to start by looking in a mirror and scoffing at ourselves, because I'm pretty sure you're like me and you've experienced more of the Israelites' response than that of Caleb and Joshua. We often choose the safety of known pain over fear of the unknown.

In an exercise of faith and sheer will, Joshua and Caleb pronounced, *"[God] will lead us into that land"* (Numbers 14:8).

Fear, unfortunately, was winning the day. In Numbers 14:10 we find out that "the whole assembly talked about stoning" Joshua and Caleb. And in the end, the fearful assembly got their wish, in a way. They didn't trek back to Egypt, but they spent another forty years (an entire generation) plunking around the desert, whining all the time:

> We will die! We are lost, we are all lost! . . . Are we all going to die? (Numbers 17:12-13)

> If only we had died when our brothers fell dead before the LORD! Why did you bring the LORD's community into this wilderness, that we and our livestock should die here? Why did you bring us up out of Egypt to this terrible place? It has no grain or figs, grapevines or pomegranates. And there is no water to drink! (Numbers 20:3-5)

Fear won. Hope lost. And of those million-plus people, only Caleb and Joshua got to enter the Promised Land, stepping into the Hope that was always there waiting for them.

## WHAT SHOULD WE DO?

You may have noticed that a couple times now I've referred to the semipermeable wall of fear. That's a good metaphorical visualization for me. When we stand open-handed before God, expressing our inability to control things and our need of Hope, we lumber into all those sticky and gooey fears. This wall isn't a fortress. It's not an edifice. It's a membrane, all slimy and grabby (moist, to use a word many tell me is their least favorite word). But it's possible—oh, yes it is—to get through it.

I have a visual imagination. And in my mind's eye, I can see this whole thing in Technicolor 3D. The zombie soul in exile, weary and emaciated, bedraggled and listless, decides that enough is enough, and it doesn't have to be this way. It shouldn't be this way. There must be something more, something that feels like Hope.

Within a few steps, this shell of a person pushes on the heavy millstone by finding some focused anger, even energy, in clarifying and articulating just what, *exactly*, it is that is dissatisfying. He struggles a bit with self-pity and blaming, but is eventually able to speak words that ring of truth about what he feels.

He steps forward, fueled by a sense of purpose, only to find himself confronted by a struggle to loosen his grip on all his attempts to control his reality. The loosening of his grip has fits and starts. It's painful, actually, since his fingers have been in that clenching position for so long. He lifts his open hands to God, looks to the mountains, and cries out in anguish, expressing the deepest longings and desires of his heart.

Then, silence. Sniffling, he considers retreating, considers clenching his hands again. But maybe a baby step forward. And in that movement he is caught in a massive membrane of fear. It has some other-worldly, sci-fi, *Aliens* goo about it. It conforms to the shape of his body and threatens to suffocate. He can move, but he can't immediately break free.

Now what?

He can pull back, gasping and choking, and run back to exile, leaving those fears and all that honesty out there in the DMZ. Or . . . or, he can exercise a force of will—faith—to stay put, to notice that he can still breathe, to wait, to name his fears.

Identifying our fears is a major factor in opening ourselves up to receive Hope. Identifying them doesn't remove them; but as I wrote earlier about my own experience, it disempowers them. When we *see* our fears, it is they who are exposed in the light. And in the light, our fears can be addressed with wisdom and speculation and curiosity ("Hey little fear, what are you about? What is it you think you need?"). Instead of *being* our fears, we move to *having* fears. We make them objective and can see them in new ways, apart from ourselves.

But our victory doesn't come from recognizing our fears, it comes from recognizing God's righteousness (all God's perfect goodness, we might say). While holding out our identified fears apart from ourselves, we welcome the righteousness of God, and our fears are defeated. This doesn't necessarily mean they go away, but they are stripped of power.

Walter Brueggemann puts it this way: "It's an embracing of God's righteousness that displaces fear."[3]

Please do not think that I'm downplaying the difficulty of what I'm suggesting. Facing our fears is not easy or simple. If it were, we wouldn't have them in the first place.

## WHAT WILL LOOKS LIKE IN THE FACE OF FEAR

In chapter four, I mentioned my friend Jon Huckins, whose work centers on training Americans in peacemaking and reconciliation by exposing them to peacemakers embedded within the Palestinian/Israeli conflict. He shared this story with me, which is such a beautiful embodiment of the courageous exercising of will in the face of fear.

My friend Daoud is a Christian Palestinian living in the West Bank with a small olive farm on a hill that's surrounded by five Jewish settlements.[4] The state of Israel does not want him or his family there. He regularly receives orders about how their land is going to be demolished.

Yet, in the middle of that, his motto is "we refuse to be enemies." When we follow the Jesus way, we can't see the other as an enemy. First and foremost, we have to see the other as a human. And so, even when we experience the worst persecution and oppression, we refuse to be enemies.

Daoud told me how he was coming back to his property one night in the old yellow Volkswagen bus he drives around the West Bank. His wife and two young children were in the vehicle with him. It was after midnight, and when he pulled up to the gate to his property, the Israeli Defense Force—the Israeli Military—stopped them. They began to hassle Daoud and ask a lot of questions.

Daoud told them, "It's late, I own this property, I live here. Can I please get in?" But they refused and ordered him out of his vehicle. So Daoud got out his vehicle to continue the conversation.

The soldiers barked, "Everyone needs to get out of the vehicle." Daoud looked them in the eye and said, "I have two young children who are sleeping in the back. If I wake them up to the sight of weapons and soldiers, they're going to have nightmares for the rest of their lives." But the soldiers rebuffed him, and Daoud was forced to wake up his children.

He went to the back of the van and leaned down to slowly

wake up his children. As he's waking them, he says—in English, so the soldiers can hear and understand, "Children, I have two friends I need you to meet."

As soon as the soldiers heard this, they were thrown off. They stepped back. They'd heard something never expected. And they let Daoud and his family through.

One of those soldiers came back weeks later and tracked down Daoud, asking, "Why did you respond like that, how could you respond like that?" Daoud explained his commitment to following Jesus, and how that leads him to a life of nonviolence. The soldier actually ended up coming back and participating on the farm with them, harvesting olives, and a friendship was birthed.

I would add that friendship wasn't the only thing birthed. Hope arrived. Hope for the soldier, and more Hope for Daoud. This was possible because Daoud had identified his own fears, disempowering them, and embraced the righteousness of God.

## DOWN IN A SNOWY PIT

Back in the Alaskan snowy pit where I was quite sure I would soon die, I'd given up. At least temporarily. I might have thought I'd rally again at some point, but I had no new plans to put into action.

But then I heard Nate's scrunch-scrunch-scrunching as he softly showshoed along. I don't know if it was intuition or delirium or a fleeting memory that I was on one of the trapping routes Nate had taken me on a few days earlier; but I called out to him. And he heard me.

Here's where the story gets both interesting and a little fuzzy in my memory. Nate hearing me wasn't enough. Nate coming over and seeing me wasn't enough. He probably even attempted to give me instructions on self-extrication. But that wasn't enough. No, Nate, able-bodied and immensely more knowledgeable about snowy pits than I was, climbed down into the pit with me. Somehow (this is the part I really don't remember, as hard as I've tried) he got me out of the pit, and back to my toasty warm cabin. (And like the seventh graders we were, we told no one, afraid of getting into trouble.)

Emmanuel, God with us, got down in here with us. In our moments of deepest and most wrenching exposure, he comes to us and meets us at the wall of fear. When Jesus shows up, fear dissipates, and Hope blooms.

## Hope Toolbox

• Which of the fears listed in this chapter—about yourself or about God—is most familiar to you and your experience? How does it manifest itself in your life?

• Mentally and emotionally put yourself back in that place of holding your honest emotions and dissatisfaction out to God in the palms of your open hands. In that space, what fears come to you most quickly? What does it feel like to identify those fears and acknowledge them before God?

• Take a few minutes to write some words about your fears. Describe them. Prayerfully consider that you *have* fear, not that you *are* fear. They're out there, on the paper or computer screen. Now, write "God's goodness" in big letters on top of your fear descriptions. Consider what you're feeling and thinking as you do this.

# SEVEN

# JESUS, THE HOPE-BRINGER

My favorite Broadway musical is *Cats.*

That's a lie, actually, and a glimpse into my strange sense of humor. Seriously, though: *Cats*? Sorry if I've offended you. Sort of.

My favorite Broadway musical is *Les Misérables.* But to be honest, I prefer the film versions because I can focus on the storyline more, not being distracted by the theatrics and staging. I was more upbeat about the 2012 version with Hugh Jackman, Anne Hathaway and Russell Crowe than many people I know. And I was two thumbs up about the 2000 version with Gérard Depardieu and John Malkovich. But my favorite version of the story, by far, is the 1998 (non-musical) version starring Liam Neeson, Geoffrey Rush, Uma Thurman and a pre-*Homeland* Claire Danes.

I think the reason the 1998 version of Les Miz is my favorite is because it contains one of my all-time favorite scenes in any film, ever. It's a scene in all versions of Les Miz, but none capture it quite like the 1998 film version.

You can skip reading this paragraph if you're a Les Miz groupie, but to make sure everyone is on the same page, *Les Misérables* is the story (written as a book by Victor Hugo in 1862, and widely considered one of the best novels of the nineteenth century) of Jean Valjean, a peasant who steals a loaf of bread for his starving sister's child and spends nineteen years in prison for the crime. After his release, he breaks parole and is hunted down by a law-obsessed police inspector named Javert. There's much more to the story, of course. It's an exploration of law and grace, loyalty, transformation and redemption.

My favorite scene occurs fairly early in the film, when Jean Valjean is first on the run for breaking parole. Turned away from multiple inns and jobs because his yellow passport marks him as a convict, Valjean is taken in for the night by a small-town priest, Bishop Myriel. During the night, Valjean steals the rectory's silver. But he is caught, and policemen return him and the stolen goods to the rectory to refute Valjean's claim that the silver was given to him, enroute to what will clearly be a return to prison.

Here's the breathtaking scene. When the police ask the bishop if the silverware is his, he responds that it *was* the rectory's, but that Valjean is correct in stating it was a gift. As the police release Valjean and turn to leave, the bishop continues, saying that Valjean had forgotten to take the silver candlesticks. Valjean's face reveals confusion, and the bishop reiterates that the valuable candlesticks were part of the gift.

Pulling Valjean aside, Bishop Myriel quietly says, "Jean Valjean, my brother, you no longer belong to evil. With this silver, I have bought your soul. I've ransomed you from fear and hatred, and now I give you back to God."

The scene is powerful to me (and thousands of others) on multiple levels.

First, I am Valjean (and so are you). I do not deserve mercy, but have been shown it countless times, by my God and by people in my life. While the punishment for Valjean's theft of bread was overly severe, he was *clearly guilty* of stealing the silver. Mercy is never deserved, or it's not mercy. All of us can resonate with the surprising fresh breeze of not receiving what we deserve.

Second, the "measure" of mercy Valjean receives is over the top: not only forgiveness, but a double-portion gift. If the story weren't so beautifully told, we might think the bishop was a little crazy, giving away the silver candlesticks to a man who'd just stolen from him. That sort of generosity doesn't align with our eye-for-an-eye thinking about justice. It's so over the top that it's completely impossible to mistakenly ascribe the gift to a legitimate response to Valjean's intrinsic goodness.

Third, this scene is a clear picture of Jesus, particularly through the lens of the bishop's final comment. Throughout the gospels we see Jesus giving when it wasn't expected, serving when it was awkward to do so, and surprising people with blessings that met their deepest longings and not only their presenting problems. In my own life, I've experienced this repeatedly also. In my desert time, I merely thought I needed help with my anxiety; but Jesus brought me Hope and life.

Finally, as a follower of Jesus, I am called to live like this, to be a dispenser of this style of mercy. Honestly, I find mercy dispensing to be simultaneously life giving and completely counter to my instincts. But I know from experience—even though it's often faltering, due to my repeated shying away from Jesus—that my very best life, the one God has always dreamed of for me, is a life of Hopecasting, an active life of carrying Hope as I interact with the world.

Ultimately, this scene in *Les Misérables* is a powerful picture of Hope's arrival. Valjean heads into the rectory courtyard, held by the policemen, completely without Hope. Full of fear and absolutely demoralized, trying to leave exile and about to be returned. He leaves with a kernel of possibility starting to crack open in his heart.

This is Jesus, who shows up in the midst of our confusion and pain and fear, and surprises us with Hope (even when we're hoping for Hope, because it's always better than what we were hoping for). Other than the fact that Valjean would not be returning to prison, the immediate circumstances of Valjean's life are still difficult. In many ways, he is still in exile. But his *imagination* is sparked, a dream of a new potential, Hope burrowing its way into his heart.

## FROM ISOLATION TO INTIMACY

After so many years, the isolation had become a mixture of normal and surreal. Like a blind person learning to navigate a home, she had developed systems and skills to make life work for her. Since she couldn't go to the market, writing out shopping lists for her daughter was second nature. Since she couldn't attend worship, she developed a routine of singing, prayer and reading in her room. Since her husband wasn't allowed to touch her, she'd settled for a relationship that felt more like being roommates. She was careful not to accidentally brush up against him, not to reach in when her son was making a mess, not to leaves clothes where anyone might accidentally step on them.

But the one thing for which she couldn't create a system was her loneliness.

She'd seen doctor after doctor to seek remedies for her twelve years of continuous menstruation. They hadn't healed her, and, in fact, had made things worse, all while bringing her family to the brink of financial ruin.

How could there be any Hope after twelve years? How could she even conceive of the idea that her exile would ever come to an end?

This story of the woman who suffered from twelve years of bleeding is told in Matthew, Mark and Luke. Growing up in church, I'd heard the story hundreds of times. But I didn't understand it, really. Until about ten years ago, I still thought it was just another story of physical healing, like the lepers and the blind that Jesus healed.

But in more recent years it has become one of my favorite Bible stories. And it has become a beacon of Hope story for me as I've learned to view Scripture through the lens I've outlined in this book. Of course, I've never experienced menstruation. For that matter, I've never experienced any illness lasting to the point where almost every aspect of my life must be rearranged to accommodate my physical challenges. On a physical level, the *only* silly comparisons I have are my colorblindness, and my faulty pancreas that demanded I not consume alcohol. Okay, not a big deal.

But the story isn't primarily about physical healing, and I find deep connection with the picture of Hope it provides.

Jewish purity laws were particularly picky about bodily fluids, including blood. As part of this reality, a menstruating woman was considered "unclean" for a week. (Wow—a week a month! What a pain!) When a good Jewish person was unclean, a whole raft of restrictions came down on them: no touching anyone; no being out in public (for fear that you might accidentally bump into someone, making them unclean); no participation in worship or attendance at temple; and a ceremonial hassle to reinstate being "clean."

I'm sure the physical problem was very real. No one can lose blood for twelve years without being put into poor health. Actually, it seems a surprise in some ways that she had even lived with this ailment for this long.

But consider her isolation. I believe that was the bigger problem, and the source of her *very real* exile.

In Luke's Gospel, he records that "no one could heal her" (Luke 8:43). In Mark's Gospel we read, "She had suffered a great deal under the care of many doctors and had spent all she had, yet instead of getting better she grew worse" (Mark 5:26). [1]

Then along comes Jesus. Apparently the woman had heard the rumors about this teacher, or rabbi, coming through town. There was plenty of buzz about him. People said he was a brilliant teacher. They said he was able to perform mind-blowing miracles, including healing the sick. Some even whispered that he might be the Messiah!

What caused her, though, to so clearly break convention? What thinking tipped the scales to the point where she was willing to risk so greatly? Maybe she had a zombie soul, and thoughts of upholding convention just didn't compute anymore. Maybe she was *just done* with being ruled by oppressive ritual. Clearly, her dissatisfaction moved her feet that day. And even though she didn't speak a word to Jesus until after he had spoken to her, the very act of reaching out to touch him was an embodied honest cry out to God.

So the woman does something bold and terrifying and absolutely rule-breaking: she leaves her house and joins the crowd. In the set-up for this story, we read a couple important framing facts. First, a temple leader named Jairus had approached Jesus for help in healing his dying daughter. This was an influential man. This was a guy who could do great things for Jesus. This was a person who could help spread the Jesus brand, create loads of viral marketing and become a celebrity endorsement for the message Jesus was trying to spread.

Second, we read that "the crowds almost crushed him" (Luke 8:42). This wasn't a sparsely populated, quiet street. This was a mob.

The woman wasn't just bold and rule-breaking in leaving her home. She was pushing her way through a sea of people, touching (*touching!*) countless who would now be ceremonially unclean. And she was interrupting what could be a turning point on the Jesus road show.

But she was desperate, and deeply dissatisfied.

She thought she was being sneaky. But she was acting with immense faith.

In Numbers 15:38, the Israelites are instructed to "make tassels on the corners of your garments, with a blue cord on each tassel." You can still see these today on the prayer shawls of Orthodox Jews.

Without going into too much detail, the tassels represent the 613 laws of Moses, by 613 knots tied into the tassels. Jesus would have been wearing one of these fringed prayer shawls.

Malachi 4:2 says, "The sun of righteousness will rise with healing in its rays," a prophetic reference to the Messiah.

But the word translated as "rays" (or "wings" in other versions) in Malachi 4:2 is the same word that's translated as "corner" (or "borders") in Numbers 15:38. As such, a good Jewish person believed that healing would be available in the corners of the prayer shawl worn by the Messiah.

We don't know for sure that the bleeding woman thought Jesus was the Messiah. But it seems very likely that she was giving it a try, seeing if the prophecy was true. Opening her grip on the normal control of her life and taking a massive risk.

She elbows her way through the crowd that was almost crushing Jesus, hoping to simply touch the tassels on the back of his garment. No one would have to know. Healing or not, she could slip in and slip out, unnoticed. People wouldn't *know* that she'd made them ritually unclean, and after touching the fringe, she could stand still and stealthily allow the crowd to flow around her, allowing her to slip on home.

But, of course, it doesn't go down that way. As soon as she touches Jesus' prayer shawl tassels, she feels instant healing. For a split second, the woman must have been euphoric, not sure whether she wanted to scream or laugh or cry or collapse of exhaustion. But then Jesus asks, "Who touched me?"

The crowd stops and immediately goes silent. They sense that something is going to happen, and they want to be sure to see it.

The woman stops in terror, afraid that she is going to be found out. She trembles, willing herself invisible. Even in the joy of her physical healing and soon-to-be-realized end of her exile, her story will humiliate her and anger everyone around her if it gets drawn out into the open.

In fact, the story tells us that when Jesus asked who touched him, they all denied it. It's that classic denial in a crowd and it's pretty funny since they were all pressing up against him, almost crushing him. If she verbalized anything at that moment, the woman probably denied touching Jesus also.

I love picturing this moment. Peter speaks up, in total frustration. He sighs and rolls his eyes, and says something like, "C'mon, Jesus. Gimme a break! Can't you see that the crowd is almost crushing you? Luke is even going to write it up that way in his Gospel someday! Of course people are touching you. Hundreds of people are touching you. And we can't stop now, man—this guy here, Jairus, could provide us with the marketing edge that will really boost our campaign! Just let it go."

All the while, the semipermeable wall of fear, that gooey membrane, is enveloping and suffocating the formerly bleeding woman.

Jesus says, "Someone touched me; I know that power has gone out from me" (Luke 8:46).

She is undone. She is physically healed, but undone. She knows she can't hide. She knows she can't get away with this, so she collapses at Jesus' feet. Trembling, crying, she pours out the whole story. The crowd back away in shock and horror, disgusted by this rule-breaker, and wonder if they've been made unclean by accidentally coming into contact with her.

Jesus responds with one of the most beautiful, gentle, intimate phrases in the entire Bible: "Daughter, your faith has healed you. Go in peace" (Luke 8:48).

Catch this: nowhere else in all of the Gospels does Jesus refer to someone as "daughter."[2] Even minutes later when he's bringing Jairus's real-life daughter back to life, he doesn't use that word. The only time Jesus is recorded calling someone daughter is with this grown woman. He uses an intimate term, a term of relationship, a term of gentle love and acceptance and the inescapability of family. The woman reached out to Jesus from exile, kept her grip open when confronted with fear and was met by the presence of Jesus. Jesus brings the woman *a faithful confidence that God is continuing to author a story.*

## IT'S NOT ME!

I am incapable of drumming up Hope in my life. So are you.

We can take on a positive outlook. We can look for the silver lining. We can choose to avoid negativity. Those are all good and healthy emotional and psychological perspectives that I try to employ, and trust you do also. But they're not enough. Only Jesus brings the sort of Hope that moves us out of exile.

Even when I cognitively acknowledge the difference between my own successes at optimism and my failures at creating Hope, my heart often tells me lies. My heart tells me that Jesus brings me Hope because he finds me worthy. And while that might be true (Jesus *does* find me worthy of his presence and Hope), my not-as-accurate spin on that devolves into thinking it's because I am *more worthy* than others who are Hope-less.

"I'm worthy" becomes "I'm deserving," but they're not the same thing. Like Valjean, I am *not* deserving; but in his mercy Jesus still finds me worthy.

I'm reminded of Tracy, a woman I never met, but whose story has had a big impact on me.

Mike Yaconelli was my friend and boss for a number of years while I worked at Youth Specialties (he tragically died in a car accident in 2003), and I'd heard him tell the story of Tracy many times in our travels together where we often spoke at the same events.[3]

Mike had long admired the wisdom of Catholic priest and author Henri Nouwen. Henri's writing had a huge impact on Mike. Though Nouwen was much more widely known than Mike, they often shared similar themes (in very different styles) in their speaking and writing.

Mike knew that Nouwen had stepped off the escalator of rising celebrity to become the priest at L'Arche Daybreak, a community for severely developmentally disabled adults in the Toronto area. That decision spoke to Mike, and he longed to spend time with Nouwen. Mike wrote Nouwen and asked if he'd be willing to lead a small spiritual retreat for Mike and his wife and a few others. Henri agreed, and Mike and seven friends headed to Toronto.

Anticipation was understandably high when they entered the room at L'Arche for their first meeting with Nouwen. They were expecting a deep and insightful time where Henri dropped pearls of wisdom into the group's waiting ears, minds and hearts. What they *weren't* expecting, however, was to have L'Arche residents in the meeting.

Tracy sat on the floor next to Mike. An adult, Tracy was so severely developmentally disabled that she couldn't speak, couldn't make eye contact and couldn't give any indication whatsoever that she understood a word being said. Tracy couldn't even sit up on her own. She had an assistant who sat on the floor behind Tracy and held Tracy between her arms and legs. Tracy constantly made groans and other sounds that were 100 percent unintelligible. Her helper had a scarf around Tracy's neck that was regularly used to wipe the drool coming out of Tracy's mouth.

We all want to think we would be compassionate and mature in a situation like this. But if we're honest (a trait Mike was uniquely known for), we would find it awkward. In fact, it was awkward *and* disappointing, since the time was clearly not going to be what Mike and his friends had been expecting.

Very early into Nouwen's first session with the group, he sensed the awkwardness in this collection of important Christian leaders. He paused, pointed at Tracy, and asked the group a no-brainer question: "Do you think Jesus loves Tracy any less than he loves you?"

It was a high lob of a question, with an easy Sunday school answer. Mike and the other leaders were all quick to respond, somewhat indignantly (sensing that Henri was suggesting they would think otherwise!), "No, of course not!"

Then Nouwen surprised them all: "And what can Tracy *do* for God?"

The correct answer of "Nothing, Tracy can't do anything for God" was obvious and unspoken in the silence that followed.

Hear this: Jesus' willingness to bring you Hope is *in no way* dependent on your service or ability or religious fervor or status or compliance or the severity of your need. Jesus' sole motivation is love.

Jesus meets us at the semipermeable wall of fear, takes our hand, and helps us step through to the other side.

See our developing diagram (fig. 7.1) of the process of Hope, reflecting the incoming movement of Jesus showing up.

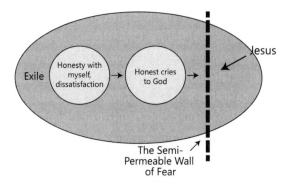

**Figure 7.1**

## THE ANNOYING SPEED OF HOPE

We live in a present-tense culture (the culture of immediacy, which I wrote about in chapter two). We're quickly losing our sense of past and future. Along with that, we're losing the learned skill of patience. We want and expect things *now*.

As a youth worker, I see this shift in the teenagers I work with. Teenagers, of course, have always found patience to be a bit of a stretch. And that makes complete sense when one considers that they're going through the most massive developmental shift they'll experience in their entire lives. But the developmentally normal desire for immediacy in teenagers has been shot with cultural steroids today. You and I live in the same culture; but those of us over forty are immigrants to this culture, and teenagers are natives; they're indigenous.

My view into the lives of young people living in the moment, however, often opens up a portal into seeing the same proclivity in my own life. When someone insists on using snail mail, I wonder if they miss the Pony Express! Just after I think, *These teenagers have completely lost all sense of patience*, I'm struck by, *Oh, to an only infinitesimally lesser degree, so have I.* And, dear reader, so have you.

Patience and slow are both in the character and practices of God.

Here are two of many scriptural references to this reality:

> The Lord is slow to anger, abounding in love and forgiving sin and rebellion. (Numbers 14:18)

> The Lord is not slow in keeping his promise, as some understand slowness. Instead he is patient with you. (2 Peter 3:9)

We *like* God's character and practice of patience and slow when it serves us. I give God regular attaboys for having patience with me.

But we chafe at God's practice of showing up with Hope on a timetable that's different than we would prefer. We'd much rather experience the abracadabra of a magician God, presto-change-o, instant Hope!

If Jesus is actively bringing Hope to my life and helping me gain imagination, both about my own future and about my future partnership with him in kingdom work, then my preference would be now, now, now. But Jesus doesn't seem to work that way—at least not most of the time. Occasionally Jesus brings Hope like a freight train, crashing into our lostness, scattering our fears and immediately ending our exile. But more often than not, the train of Hope comes into the station slowly, and by our timetables, late. I want out immediately, want instant rescue; but it seems I'm being asked to exercise patience.

This tension takes me back to the question of motivation. Why doesn't Jesus drop some pixie dust on my life and change it all in an instant? I'm left with two good options, sequential in their priority:

The motivation for everything Jesus does is love.

The slow, patient journey of Hope must be the route and timetable that is in my best interest, since love is the motivation for its selection.

When I asked Gary Haugen of International Justice Mission how he was able to find Hope while investigating the Rwandan genocide, he told me, "Hope really is in the character of God. I had to ask myself, 'Who's in charge of this reality? Is it totally random? If someone's in charge, what's his character?'" That sure sounds like *a faithful confidence that God continues to author a story.*

## HOPE, JESUS, RESURRECTION AND HEAVEN

Any book about Christian Hope, and any chapter about Jesus and Hope, has to address the issue of heaven, as it's both deeply connected to Hope and so commonly misunderstood.

While readying myself to write this book, I read a handful of books on hope—mostly books about the theology of hope and biblical teaching on hope. But I also perused Amazon, looking at dozens or hundreds of books written at a more popular level, trying to give Christians an understanding of hope. And what I found surprised me: the bulk of the Christian books on hope all focus on hope being connected, exclusively, to the afterlife. While the resurrection plays a central role, undoubtedly, the sole focus on the afterlife as the reason for hope is not a biblical idea.

Countless books and even more sermons about hope say mostly the same thing: *Life sucks; but have hope, because one day Jesus is going to take us away from this hell hole to a better place.*

I have so many problems with this pervasive line of thinking I hardly know where to begin. I suppose it should be enough that the idea isn't biblical. And I am not fond of the image of God that message portrays, as if God is saying: *Suck it up. I know my creation is vastly disappointing to you—it is to me also! But hold on for as long as you can currently imagine, because I've got something swell planned for you after you finish your mediocre, unfulfilling time on Earth, or what the angels sometimes cheekily refer to as "the beta test."*

As much as those problems get stuck in my craw, the more gritty source of my opposition to the "hope is exclusively about the afterlife" line of thinking is that it really doesn't offer me much for today. You and I live now. And we need a Hope that gets us out of bed in the morning. We need a Hope that shifts our social imagination for *this* world, and *this* life, and *this* day. If we're all going to leave this place behind to burn, why bother? Why engage in anything good? Why search for meaning, or to impart meaning to others? Why stand against injustice? Other than the idea of "saving souls," why not merely fire up the Xbox, grab a bag of Cool Ranch Doritos and wait for the end?

The biblical teaching about heaven and the afterlife has been written about in plenty of other places—for me, most clearly in N. T. Wright's *Surprised by Hope: Rethinking Heaven, the Resurrection, and the Mission of the Church.*[4] I don't intend for this book to focus on the afterlife or heaven. But since it's the pervasive understanding of what Jesus and the Bible teach about hope, it seems wise to at least briefly go there.

In short, Jesus' teaching about the afterlife—and the rest of the Bible is strongly congruent with this—is that he was inaugurating a new reality where the kingdom of heaven was coming to the earth. Notice the direction of that movement: it's Jesus bringing the kingdom of heaven *to us*, in our here and now. This is the same movement, the same direction and the same provider of Hope: brought *to us*, by Jesus, in our here and now.

The idea that our souls, or spirits, or some "essence" of who we are, will move on to an otherworld in the sky leaving our physical bodies behind is the misinformed focus of most funeral sermons. That line of thinking has much more to do with Plato and his theory of dualism—that spirit is good and matter is evil—than Jesus or the Bible.

The focus of Jesus' teaching on Hope, heaven and the afterlife was about redemption and resurrection. This was a revolutionary idea to *all* the ears listening to him teach: Jewish, Roman and Greek.

In all religions and myths, the primary difference between god(s) and humans is immortality. That issue seems to be the thread of so many stories: finite, mortal (a word that means *doomed to die*) humans want immortality (a word that means *deathlessness*). And while the gods were immortal, humans looked for loopholes or favors that would move them from mortal to immortal.

The ancient Greeks believed that formerly mortal humans like Achilles and Helen of Troy were granted immortality by the intervention of the gods.

Sir Galahad, one of Arthur's knights, was believed to achieve immortality after finding the Holy Grail.

Merlin the magician was, in some stories, said to be trapped in a cave, or a tomb, or a mist indefinitely. Not exactly an immortality party, but immortality nonetheless.

Others didn't make the move from mortal to immortal, but were simply considered immortal all along, even though they lived in human bodies.

Ancient Egyptian pharaohs were believed to be divine (and, therefore, immortal).

Chinese emperors were considered "Sons of Heaven," all the way up to 1911!

Roman emperor Julius Caesar was pronounced a deity in 42 B.C., referred to as "The Divine Caesar." And his son, Caesar Augustus, was called "Son of the Divine One." Augustus was emperor when Jesus was born.

Our human thirst for immortality shows up often in fiction, in works as disparate as *The Lord of the Rings*, *Star Trek*, *Harry Potter* and all the vampire fiction bloating the young adult section of your neighborhood bookstore.

We humans have plenty of problems. But death seems to be the biggest, most pervasive, most obsession-focused universal giant.

Jesus' incarnation—coming to earth to live as a human—is one of my favorite things about the Christian faith. It's beautiful and challenging and provocative. It encourages my outlook and forms my thoughts and practices about ministry. But at the risk of sounding like I'm lessening its importance (I'm not), the idea of a god coming to earth to walk among humans is not unique to our story. Most faiths—including hundreds of now defunct religions and myths of antiquity—

have some aspect of the divine taking on human form for visiting hours.

But the death and resurrection parts of the Jesus story, those are unique.

Jesus' death, among other extremely important purposes, is a natural extension of the beauty and mystery of the incarnation: God choosing to become limited in order to become one of us (there's the *to us* movement direction again). Jesus' identification with us wouldn't be complete if he hadn't also experienced the one thing that humans so desperately and universally fear: death. God died. The eternally preexisting persons of the Trinity experienced loss and separation. The God of relationship experienced, in a real and tangible way, a break of intimacy.

And Jesus' "I am with you" reality gets flipped around in the resurrection. Jesus, already identifying with us all the way to death, invites us to continue that connection via resurrection.[5] Jesus' bodily resurrection isn't only a show of power and victory over death, it's an offer of what humans have longed for from the beginning of time: immortality. In relationship, Jesus reaches out his hand and says, "Do you want to live forever? Good, I want you to live forever also."

I've previously referenced Paul's famous words about Hope in Romans 8:24-25:

> For in this hope we were saved. But hope that is seen is no hope at all. Who hopes for what they already have? But if we hope for what we do not yet have, we wait for it patiently.

But look at the also-famous verses that immediately precede Paul's words about Hope:

> I consider that our present sufferings are not worth comparing with the glory that will be revealed in us. For the creation waits in eager expectation for the children of God to be revealed. For the creation was subjected to frustration, not by its own choice,

but by the will of the one who subjected it, in hope that the creation itself will be liberated from its bondage to decay and brought into the freedom and glory of the children of God.

We know that the whole creation has been groaning as in the pains of childbirth right up to the present time. Not only so, but we ourselves, who have the firstfruits of the Spirit, groan inwardly as we wait eagerly for our adoption to sonship, the redemption of our bodies. (Romans 8:18-23)

Creation waits. Not for us to *leave*, but for liberation.

The whole of creation, currently subject to bondage and decay, will be brought into freedom.

But Jesus doesn't merely continue existing as a spirit, slipping off in the ether back to heaven. Jesus was physically resurrected.

And we are offered that same resurrection.

Yes, I absolutely believe in a real afterlife—heaven. And since I, along with pretty much every human who has ever lived, like the idea of immortality (deathlessness) more than mortality (doomed to die), I'm very much down with Jesus' offer.

But Hope—the present day, gritty sort, the get out of bed variety, the re-sparked imagination of a new reality version, the joining up with Jesus in his restoration of all creation kind—is so much more wonderful than a ticket to board the Heaven Express. Instead, when it comes to Jesus and our future, Hope is connected to resurrection and continually living in the kingdom of God. After all, Jesus didn't talk about a one-day kingdom of God: he inaugurated it. And if the kingdom of God is here and how, then I want to get moving and participate in some restoration!

Once, on being asked by the Pharisees when the kingdom of God would come, Jesus replied, "The coming of the kingdom of God is not something that can be observed, nor will people say,

'Here it is,' or 'There it is,' because the kingdom of God is in your midst." (Luke 17:20-21)

# Hope Toolbox

- It's difficult to reflect on Jesus' role in bringing you Hope if you don't have a somewhat clear sense of who Jesus was and is. So take a moment to prayerfully and honestly consider your views about Jesus. Intentionally avoid the answers you think you're *supposed* to give, and just be bluntly honest (Jesus is fine with this, by the way). It might be helpful to think in the two categories of "Who Jesus *was*" and "Who Jesus *is*."

- What's your honest reaction to the reality that Jesus' restoration of our lives and our Hope is usually a long and slow process? If his motivation is love, why might Jesus choose that timetable? Ask God to give you patience (it's a fruit of the Holy Spirit, after all).

- If it's true that Jesus' rescue isn't about taking you away to *some other place* after you die, but is—as the Bible teaches—about restoring and transforming all things, what implications does that have for how you live and the choices you make? What difference does it make if you have *Hope for today* instead of only *hope about the afterlife*?

# HOPE'S ARRIVAL

In chapter one I shared stories of my perspective-altering trip to Haiti mere weeks after the earthquake in 2010. Three months later, I went back again.

I'd been in conversations with the missions organization that had hosted my first trip (the one with the youth workers) about what we'd seen and experienced. One thing had been very clear to us: God's Spirit was moving in Haiti, and the Haitian church seemed to be waking up from a deep, long slumber. This is completely my observation (informed by conversations with Haitian church leaders), and not the definitive conclusion of cultural and missiological study, but the pre-earthquake Haitian church had been meek and the post-earthquake Haitian church was bold. And with so little infrastructure in place (even *before* the earthquake, but particularly *after*), we saw that resourcing Haitian church leaders in their vision for meeting the physical, emotional and spiritual needs of their fellow citizens would have further reaching impact than anything we could create ourselves.

We developed a church partnership program, where an American church could partner directly with a Haitian church for specific, contextual and strategic resourcing, prayer and development. And in an attempt to get the word out about this opportunity, I took a unique collection of social media–savvy American church leaders with me to explore the idea. My hope was that some of them would find a long-term partnership, and that all of them would spread the word.

I also had a personal agenda. My own church had, I felt, a very limited worldview. I loved (still do) my church and all its passion and quirkiness. But I regularly felt that our vision was *exclusively* for Judea, and not for Samaria or the ends of the earth. So I invited Ed, my church's brand-new senior pastor (he'd been the teaching pastor for ten years prior to this role change), to come along. I say this was "selfish" because he really didn't fit the criteria of who we were inviting on the trip—he didn't have a social media platform or followers around the country. His one point of influence was with our own church.

After a few days of seeing the damage in Port-au-Prince, hearing hundreds of stories, visiting and problem solving with leaders in makeshift tent cities, and a variety of other exposure experiences, we were all pretty worn out. And it probably wasn't great timing when, the day before we were to fly home, I mentioned to the missions leader that we didn't seem to have a mechanism in place for trip participants to have conversations with the pastors of potential partner churches. He agreed, and rallied. That evening was one of the more awkward missions experiences I've ever had. (I don't blame the missions leader for this at all. He was scrambling to meet my request, on my terms. I take full responsibility.)

Since our group was exhausted, and it wasn't practical to drive all over Port-au-Prince to meet a few dozen pastors in their own churches, they all came to us. The word was put out through a local network of Haitian church pastors, and two or three dozen showed up at our little guesthouse that evening for what can only be described as missionary speed dating.

Each of our team participants settled into a couch or up to a table, and a parade of Haitian pastors cycled through, having five- to ten-minute meetings. I'm embarrassed by this, I must say, because it set everyone up to live into the worst stereotypes: us, the benevolent providers, screening potential suitors who were, in turn, forced to sell themselves to us as the most worthy recipients. That truly wasn't our intent, but it sure felt icky.

Ed and I sat in a corner of the living room and met with eager pastor after eager pastor. It all felt wrong, and the meetings were predictably unfruitful. Good-hearted Haitian pastors shared their vision with us, but each one felt like he was making it up on the spot, sure that we were looking for something.

Part of the problem was we didn't really know what we were looking for. We were just hoping that God would be obvious, that we would be able to discern when the fit was right.

At some point, the speed dating wound down, and Ed and I returned to our room, completely discouraged and a little bit confused. We'd both felt like God had something for us here, but we'd never even sensed that God was in the room. We started debriefing (the day and our bodies!), talking each other into waiting, since the timing didn't seem right.

Then came a knock on the door of the room six of us were sharing. There was one more pastor who'd just showed up, late. Could we come down and meet with him, just to be polite?

I don't mean to overdramatize this, but the very second we walked into the room where Pastor Edouard was standing, *everything* felt different. Even before any of us spoke a word, the room was pulsating. It felt like life, and electricity, and warmth, and goodness, and potential. It felt like *Hope*.

Still before words were spoken, Ed and I looked at each other and nonverbally—wide-eyed—communicated that we were sensing the same thing.

Pastor Edouard was a spitfire in a tiny package. Older than both of us, he seemed to have more vitality and vision than the two of us combined. And *he* started to question *us*. It was awesome. We were on our heels immediately, almost giggling as we responded to his questions about our intent. He wasn't looking for a handout. His God was powerful enough to meet the needs of his community without us. He was looking for a community of believers that his church could bless through prayer, friendship and mutual involvement.

And when we asked about his vision for his church and community (in Carrefour, by the way—a suburb of Port-au-Prince and the epicenter of the earthquake), he shared with us plans he'd been holding, in hope and expectation, for multiple years. For example, he wanted to provide an inexpensive medical clinic for his community, which was more needed now than ever. And he'd been paying the rent on a nearby property for three years out of his own pocket, dreaming that it could become this clinic. But he didn't have the means to realize his dream, and had continued waiting on God.

Ed and I knew, with absolute clarity and deep conviction, that we wanted to hold up Pastor Edouard's arms when he was weary, just as Aaron and Hur had done for Moses when he grew tired while the Israelites defended themselves against invaders. And in hindsight, I can see—especially as my church has gotten to know Edouard over these past four years—that he embodies the very process I've outlined in this book. He and the people in his community had experienced exile; he was very clear about his dissatisfaction with the way things are; he had honestly cried out to God, opening his hands of control and exposing himself to the unknown; and he had faced multiple fears along the way, questioning his leadership and the vision he felt God had given him, wondering if God would come through. And in the midst of that struggle, Edouard exerted *will*, leaning into faith that God's gift of Hope would arrive. Get this: Ed and I weren't that gift. We weren't (and aren't) Hope. Edouard already *possessed* Hope when we walked into that little guesthouse sitting room. Hope had arrived for him amidst his sorrow and pain and his struggle with the membrane of fear.

Edouard's Hope, his faithful confidence that God is continuing to author a story—something he didn't manufacture or force into reality, something much greater than optimism or wishful thinking—has deeply impacted thousands in Carrefour, Haiti, and an equal number at my church in La Mesa, California. For Edouard, Hope isn't just a positive feeling. Hope isn't limited to a better outlook. Hope has taken him from vision to action.

With Jesus, Hope intrinsically, unwaveringly enters into our lives. Where Jesus is, Hope is also. So our diagram now looks like this:

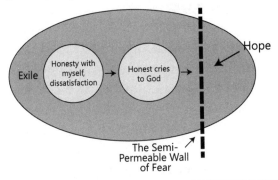

**Figure 8.1**

## WEE ZACCHAEUS MEETS HOPE

A short guy with a big case of little man syndrome, Zacchaeus was one of the most powerful men in town. As the chief tax collector and superintendent of customs, he was triply rich and powerful. All tax collectors were assumed to be wealthy, because they made their living by capriciously adding whatever little extra they thought they could get away with on top of the taxes imposed by the Roman oppressors they worked for. This wasn't a secretive practice: it was state-sponsored extortion. But Zacchaeus was also the chief tax collector, at the top of a mafia-like collection syndicate with trickle-up, under the table envelopes filled with cash. And he plied this trade in Jericho, the center for the production and export of balsam, a highly valuable resin gum used in both medicines and expensive perfumes.

Tax collector = rich.

Chief tax collector = doubly rich.

Chief tax collector in Jericho = triply rich.

But he was also triply hated, triply exiled. As a Jew, he was seen as the worst sort of sell-out, a collaborator with the Roman oppressors, who added insult to injury for his own selfish gain.

Jews despised tax collectors. Case in point: when Jesus was giving instructions on how to handle offenses against oneself (recorded by Matthew, a former tax collector himself), he said to talk to the person first, then take a couple witnesses and talk again, then take the matter before the church; *then*, if they are still not responsive, "treat them as you would a pagan or a tax collector" (Matthew 18:17). In other words, separate yourself from them completely. Stay away.

The Pharisees—who we tend to think of as pious dirtbags, but were really the most devoutly religious people of their time—believed that the Messiah would not return until all the Jews were living righteously (which to them meant "religiously"). They saw tax collectors as a prime example for why the Messiah had not yet come.

Jesus walks through Jericho one day, and the buzz is electric. People line the streets to see this rabbi who has rumors flying. Is he a prophet? A magician? Some, cautiously, are even whispering the word "Messiah." Think of this from Zacchaeus's perspective: *This is MY town. I'm important and powerful here. And nothing happens in my town that I'm not aware of.*

Plenty of writers ascribe all sorts of good and pure and noble motives to Zacchaeus's little scramble up the sycamore fig tree (his name, somewhat ironically, does mean "pure and righteous one"). Matthew Henry's commentary, an eighteenth-century expositional treatise still widely in use today, reflects: "Those who sincerely desire a sight of Christ, like Zaccheus, will break through opposition, and take pains to see him."[1]

I don't think it's that neat and tidy. Those interpretations subtly imply that it was Zacchaeus's goodness, or at least his good behavior, that caused Jesus to reorganize his day planner. It wasn't Zacchaeus's goodness that brought him into Jesus' sight line; it was his lostness. But here's what I find both fascinating and instructive: Zacchaeus, knowingly or unknowingly, *was* actively positioning himself for an encounter with Jesus.

Here's where my imagination takes me on this one: Zacchaeus had experienced the crisis of exile and he didn't like it. He was powerful and wealthy, but as is common for people of power and wealth, he was lonely. He was forced to keep people at a distance (even subordinate tax collectors) in order to maintain his control.

But powerful and wealthy people who are in control don't run ahead and climb a sycamore fig tree in order to get a view. That's out of control behavior, undignified, awkward, even laughable.

It seems much more likely that we're catching Zacchaeus in the process of moving toward Hope, even though it likely wasn't his intention. In order to get to the point where he was willing to make a fool of himself, he must have experienced some sort of dissatisfaction with who he was, or what he'd done, or his place in life. Maybe it's a little stretch, but climbing that tree sure sounds like the physical equivalent of an honest cry to God.

Imagine him up in that tree, holding on, trying not to allow a breeze to blow up his tunic and create an embarrassing "wee little man" sighting. He's exposed. He's out of control (in other words, he has given up control). But I have to believe that in that moment, his only plan is to *see*, not to *be seen*. Zacchaeus was likely horrified at the idea of being seen.

Jesus stops and turns his head. The crowd noise lowers, as everyone cranes their necks in an attempt to follow the line from Jesus' gaze to ...what? ... the chief tax collector up a tree?

In that moment between Jesus looking at him and Jesus speaking to him, what do you think Zacchaeus was feeling? Come on, it had to be the form-fitting stickiness of fear.

> *He's going to call me out and condemn me.*
> *He's going to expose me for the fraud that I am.*
> *Everyone's going to laugh at me, and I'll lose social status and influence.*
> *My coworkers will chuckle about this for years to come, and it will be that awkward silence of the interrupted story when I walk into the room.*
> *If I could just slither down this tree trunk and slink away, back to exile, things would be better.*

But Jesus does something shockingly audacious. We know Jesus, so the story doesn't have the punch for us that the real-life action would have carried. We know Jesus is pure love, and we know the outcome of the story. But Jesus *even speaking* to Zacchaeus was unorthodox. Suggesting that they have dinner together, in Zacchaeus's house— well, that broke every social convention, and went off like a landmine under the assumptions of what the Messiah would or should do. A good Jew *does not* eat with sinners, and Zacchaeus was the worst of the worst!

Zacchaeus is clearly ripe and ready, perfect fruit in the tree, waiting for a rescue from his exile, his dissatisfaction, his fear. With eleven little words—"Zacchaeus, come down immediately. I must stay at your house today" (Luke 19:5)—Jesus comes to Zacchaeus's wall of fear, meets him there and exhales a giant puff of Hope into Zacchaeus's life.

The change in Zacchaeus is, of course, massive. He calls Jesus "Lord." He instantly commits (maybe even over-zealously?) that he'll give half of everything he owns to the poor, and pay back everyone he's cheated at 400 percent. Jesus declares that salvation has come to Zacchaeus. But Jesus isn't saying, "Guess what, Zacchaeus? You get to go to heaven someday!" No, Jesus is pronouncing rescue over Zacchaeus's life.

At that moment, was Zacchaeus still hated? Absolutely.

Did he still have a major life mess to deal with? More than ever.

Were all his problems solved? Nope.

So what changed?

Delivery for Mr. Zacchaeus: Jesus sent you an enormous box of Hope. And that special delivery of Hope moved Zacchaeus into action.

## THE PARTNERSHIP OF HOPE

Once Hope starts to arrive with the presence of Jesus, what does the change in our lives look like? How does the "moving out of exile" begin to manifest itself? Our definition of Hope is *a faithful confidence that God continues to author a story that moves us from vision to action.* So what's that "moves us from vision to action" part look like?

The tiny organization I co-lead is a partnership between me and another guy—Adam McLane. We've grown a smidge in the last year, and have other people working with us now. But particularly early on, when it was just the two of us, the partnership was extremely amoeba-like, shape shifting and morphing constantly.

The vast majority of our work in those early days wasn't very obviously parceled out to Adam's skill set or mine. I'd start something, and he would improve it, and we'd both promote it. Or he would pitch me a brilliant idea, and I'd flesh it out on paper and beta test it a bit, and we'd have a meeting to decide who was going to carry what aspects of the workload. We found coworking in the same space to be essential (often on shared Google docs even when we were three feet from each other).

With the arrival of Hope, we're invited into partnership with God. And our partnership with God in the Hope-filled restoration of our lives (and our world) looks very much the same. Certainly, there are some things that *only* God can do. And God has made you wonderfully unique in experience and personality and strengths so you are best suited for some portions of the new reality. But most of the action leading toward a new life isn't God working in one corner and you working in another; most of it is a bumping-into-each-other active partnering.[2]

God brings a seed of vision, and you exercise the discipline to notice it. God invites you to put words to it, then pokes at your heart to help you sand down rough edges and refine it. God brings power and you bring sweat. God brings roadblocks and surprisingly open doors, and you beta test, experimenting with the working out. This shouldn't imply that the give-and-take between you and God is worked out exclusively in a prayer closet or time of meditation. It's a process most often worked out *in action*, as your choices and behaviors and language and attempts at living with Hope interact with a gracious, giving, invitational God.

And in the midst of that active partnership, your Hope grows and grows—the train pulls fully into the station. Your *desires* get clarified, your *anticipation* grows, and you find yourself *cherishing* the whole process. In fact, you just might find that cherishing the partnership becomes more life giving and sustaining and transforming than your previously assumed need for an arrival at a completed state.

This is why people who have a life of struggle, by all external measurements, can still be our most shining examples of a life of Hope. It's not that they've become content (with illness, or financial challenges, or relational disappointment), it's that they've come to prioritize a partnership with God in the midst of struggle more than a resolved place of pain-free arrival.

In Haiti, Pastor Edouard's life absolutely remains full of struggle—even dissatisfaction. But he is an embodiment of Hope because he is daily partnering with God in bringing salvation. Zacchaeus most certainly had many years of challenges ahead of him—the loss of easy income, complicated relationships, follow through on his promises to repay—but that evening with Jesus started a partnership, I have to believe. And that partnership both intensified and gave shape to the Hope in Zacchaeus's life.

In my own time of deep loss, Jesus came to me in the desert. And in the weeks that followed, new ideas for my future started gushing through me. Were they God's ideas, or were they my ideas? Really, I'm not sure. And, ultimately, it doesn't matter. I started partnering with God in actualizing something new. And the process did more than bring relief to my anxiety: it converted Hope from a vision to action and got me moving out of exile.

## THIRD ISAIAH

Back in chapter two, I wrote about how scholars consider the Old Testament book of Isaiah to have three distinct parts. Sometimes these are even referred to as First, Second and Third Isaiah. First Isaiah explains how Judah got into the mess of exile, and Second Isaiah laments the misery of exile.

But there's a significant shift between chapter 55 and 56 in Isaiah, and chapters 56–66 have an entirely new message *and* tone. Instead of lamenting, Isaiah now paints a picture of a new, hopeful potential. Old Testament scholar Walter Brueggemann calls this an "unleashing of social imagination."

Look at the hopeful, partnering-with-God language of this familiar verse:

Since ancient times no one has heard,
  no ear has perceived,
no eye has seen any God besides you,
  who acts on behalf of those who wait for him. (Isaiah 64:4)

That's not the language of lament! That's Hope-talk, baby! Notice a few very important truths about that beautiful verse:

Isaiah does *not* connect God's provision to the people behaving properly, being good boys and girls.

But Isaiah *does* connect God's provision to the people's willingness to wait.

And there is no hint of "maybe" or "sometimes" in this verse. There's no wishful thinking. God's over-the-top action (never before seen or heard of in any other god!) is a future-tense statement of fact.

Most current-day pastors or theologians reflecting on Hope must sooner or later interact with the theological work of Jürgen Moltmann. Moltmann, in his exhaustive (and exhausting!) *Theology of Hope*, writes:

> Hopes and anticipations of the future are not a transfiguring glow superimposed upon a darkened existence, but are realistic ways of perceiving the scope of our real possibilities, and as such they set everything in motion and keep it in a state of change.[3]

That's what Third Isaiah provides for the Israelites: a hopeful statement of reality about what our lives *will be*. It's a clarion call to *imagine* (using Brueggemann's word[4]) the future God prepares even now, against all odds or current indications.

That's what I long for, for you and for me. Honestly, it's what I think I've been experiencing in these last few years. A transfiguring glow superimposed upon my darkened reality is okay, I guess. I mean, glowy stuff sounds fun—sort of like a lava lamp in my gloomiest days. But so much better than a glow—YES!—is my perception of the scope of real possibilities. Wishful thinking is the lava lamp glow. Hope is imagination about my very real future that I can begin stepping into.

Interesting, isn't it, that Moses himself—the patriarch of exiles—experiences a bit of glow. After the exodus, when Moses met with God on Mt. Sinai, he came back with the radiance of God glowing from his face. Surely, this was quite a sight to see. And while it amazed the people, Moses' glow-in-the-dark face became a bit of an issue also.

The glow wasn't enough. Moses took to wearing a veil over his face (so manly!) so people couldn't see the glow fading.

In contrast, Paul writes about our Hope, which is better than a glow-in-the-dark face:

> And we all, who with unveiled faces contemplate the Lord's glory, are being transformed into his image with ever-increasing glory, which comes from the Lord, who is the Spirit. (2 Corinthians 3:18)

---

# Hope Toolbox

- Can you think of a time when Jesus *did* bring Hope into your life? What were the circumstances surrounding that experience? In what shape or sense or means did Hope materialize (provision, help, a new perspective, peace)?

- Spend a minute reflecting on our definition of Hope: *Hope is faithful confidence that God continues to author a story that moves us from vision to action.* What words or ideas jump out to you? What implications does this have for your life, immediately, and for your future?

- How might you reach out and receive Hope in a way that moves "from vision to action"? What tangible action steps would you take?

---

# NINE

# HOPE'S DANCE PARTNER

*Transformed Longings*

When we're in exile, our longings are naturally self-focused (*I need this to stop!*). Being honest with ourselves about our dissatisfaction is an expression of these self-focused longings. And when we honestly cry out to God, releasing control, we're holding our longings out in the palms of our hands. So what happens to our longings once Hope arrives and starts moving us, in partnership with God, out of exile? Do our longings simply cease to exist? No, I don't think they do. Instead, I believe our longings are transformed.

Over the last dozen years, I've had the truly wonderful opportunity to travel to Argentina more than ten times. These trips were always hosted by Especialidades Juveniles, a youth ministry organization active all over the Spanish-speaking world, for me to speak at their youth worker training events. Over those many trips, I have explored the amazing city of Buenos Aires multiple times, even growing comfortable with finding my own way around the city center to restaurants and other sites that became favorites over time.

On two occasions, both at the suggestion of traveling companions, I attended a tango dinner theater. Honestly, I'm not normally much of a ballroom dancing fan. I've never had any desire to watch *Dancing with the Stars* or any similar television show. When my daughter was young, I sat bored and uncomfortable in the back of countless dance competitions, proud of my kid and there to support her, but otherwise queasy with the forced pageantry, shuffling around with the other dads who just wanted to find a sports bar in which to hide.

But the tango, well, it's a unique and memorable dance, especially when performed with expertise and passion in the country where it was invented.

Here's how one dance studio's website describes tango:

> Tango is earthy and dramatic. Although walking movements dominate, tango walks, having a "stalking" or "sneaking" character, are unlike the walks of other ballroom dances. Movements are sometimes slow and slithery, and other times sharp and staccato, such as a quick foot flick or a sharp head snap to promenade position. Tango has the same counterclockwise flow of movement around the dance floor, but with a lesser sense of urgency in comparison to the smoother and more continuous ballroom dances.[1]

The tango is romantic, even decadent. It's passionate, fluid and dynamic. The two dancers are inseparable, and constantly move—slither, even—in a give-and-take synergistic flow.

Tango, in my mind, is the perfect visualization of the dance between Hope and longing.

Once we pass through the semipermeable wall of fear, with our zombie souls sparking to the Hope-gift brought by Jesus, we move into partnership with God. But that partnership has in its sights a new reality that is not yet fully realized.

The apostle Paul famously puts it this way:

> Who hopes for what they already have? But if we hope for what we do not yet have, we wait for it patiently. (Romans 8:24-25)

Hope *always* has a continued sense of longing inseparably linked to its side. Even the encyclopedia entry on hope acknowledges this reality: "When hope has attained its object, it ceases to be hope and becomes possession."[2] And Webster's list of hope synonyms hints at this reality with *anticipate, await, watch for.*[3]

Hope is not a destination point. What we really long for is the new reality. Hope isn't that reality; Hope is the life-giving fuel that both keeps us moving and invites us into further interaction with God, moving us from vision to action.

When I was still very young by today's average marriage ages— twenty-one years old—I knelt down in the aisle of a chapel that had great spiritual importance to me and asked Jeannie to marry me. What came next, after her "Yes," was a period of hope and longing that carried all the way *through* the actual wedding ceremony. I was very much looking forward to the wedding, and played an active role in its planning. But it wasn't really the actual wedding ceremony that I longed for. It wasn't "getting married" that I wanted. It was marriage to Jeannie. The wedding itself was a wonderful moment of hope, to be sure, but longing was still present, longing for a lifetime of *being married* to her.

A wedding ceremony is a great metaphor for the relationship between Hope and longing. Hope arrives, often at a very specific point in time. But in reality, the wedding is just the opening notes of the tango.

Some talk about the kingdom of God as a "now and not yet" or "already and not yet" dual reality.[4] A wedding has that sense—already married (by the end of the ceremony), but not yet living a day-to-day married life together. Hope has that same sense: already something new, already a rescue, already Jesus entering into my mess, already new vision, but still longing for the full embodiment of living in the Promised Land.

So, if longing is always a tango partner of Hope, we would be wise to think about longing as a good and helpful gift also.

## THE GIFT OF LONGING

My friend Tessa (not her real name) had a hellacious year and a half, losing a marriage, a job, a home, her health and much more in the span of months. With those losses, the future she envisioned was shattered.

Less than two years ago, Tessa and her husband were partnered in running his small contracting business. Cash flow was tough at times, but they were making it work. And while there were surely strains in their marriage, a future together—along with their teenage daughter—was assumed.

Then, seemingly out of the blue, her husband indicated that he wasn't sure about their future together. And there seemed to be another woman in the picture. On a day reminiscent of the biblical Job, a day you wouldn't wish on your worst enemy, Tessa got news of two things: Her husband was leaving, and she had a bone tumor in her leg. Days later, she found out the tumor was cancerous.

Suddenly, in a matter of a week or two, Tessa found herself in an upside-down world:

An unemployed single mother,

with cancer,

and no insurance,

struggling through the emotions of being deserted,

having no income,

no savings,

and dealing with a social services world that would take months to get her any real help.

There was no immediate salvation, and things only got worse. Tessa struggled to find a place to live since she couldn't afford her rented home anymore and her husband wasn't providing any financial support. She applied for more than a hundred menial jobs but got nowhere, partially because the bone cancer in her leg meant she couldn't be on her feet. She had horrible credit since she and her husband had gone through bankruptcy a few years earlier. She got food stamps, but only had enough to keep her daughter fed so Tessa hardly ate and lost a dangerous amount of weight off her already thin body.

When we talked about Hope and longing, Tessa told me, "When I had a late-term miscarriage five years ago, I told a friend, 'I packed up my heart, and refuse to hope ever again.' She gave me a little basket, and told me I should put notes in it about things that give me hope, or things I hope for. I refused to put anything in it all these years. I had hoped in so many things that didn't come through. I think I'd concluded that God's hope and my hope just didn't align."

Sounds like downtown exile: separated from relationships and health and all assumptions of a positive future. As is always the case with exile, there seemed to be no pathways back to Hope, and no rescue in sight.

As the months passed, Tessa had surgery to remove the cancerous tumor, working through the nightmare of public health agencies. Months of recuperation further prevented getting work. Her ex-husband provided small amounts of cash on a couple occasions, but they didn't amount to much more than a fraction of child support (a year into her exile, the courts were still not enforcing any consistent financial support). Tessa is a strong and resourceful woman, but her strength and resourcefulness weren't enough.

In her exile, Tessa realized she had a growing sense of "I don't matter." This suspicion grew into a belief. Beyond the presenting issues of poverty and poor health and constant struggle, the deeper dissatisfaction was a conviction that she didn't matter to anyone—even to God.

She told me, "When my husband left, I was told I didn't matter, not only for love and commitment, but also for child and spousal support. I didn't matter enough to the social worker to make things happen. I didn't matter enough to my family to cosign on a loan for me. I was told, 'You *should* have had a career, you *should* do this or have done that. You're a privileged white American woman with a degree. You should be completely able to make this work.' And if none of that ever happened, I wanted to know if I mattered to God."

With that in mind, Tessa planned her own suicide. In my thinking, suicide is both a result of exile and a completely hopeless act of permanently exiling oneself.

It was early evening on Halloween, and she planned to take her life that night. Her daughter came home from school in her Halloween costume. It involved some makeup that had been poorly applied by dad's new girlfriend. When Tessa made a casual comment about how the makeup could have been better, her daughter started crying (which Tessa said she never did). Her daughter told Tessa that she had wanted Tessa to do her makeup.

Tessa told me, "I realized I couldn't leave her. It was a little spark of 'I matter.'

"Being important to my daughter got me through that weekend, but I longed to know I mattered beyond that. I asked myself, 'What if I somehow lost my daughter?' I knew my need to matter was existential—I needed to matter beyond all reason.

"It took me a year to figure that out—scraping by and trying the next thing. Leaning on friends. Friends made me eat, paid for things, provided for me, let me and my daughter move in.

"I started being able to hold on to miniature versions of 'I matter,' little gifts of hope. I had to *choose* to receive the gifts that led me toward hope, even if the gifts weren't what I would have asked for or expected. I had to let go of my expectations and definitions of satisfaction and what people *should* offer or give."

One day, Tessa ran into the pastor of the church she'd started attending. She tried to avoid him, but wasn't able to. When he genuinely asked how she was doing (not really knowing most of her story), she chose honesty. Later that week they met, and he asked her, "In five words or less, what do you want?"

"I want to experience peace," was her response.

She told me, "Nothing outside of me was going to fix this fear inside of me that I didn't matter. I realized I didn't have peace because I didn't feel that I mattered. That was my deepest fear: that I don't and never will matter to anyone."

I told Tessa that I'd wanted to talk with her about her experience because I could see Hope budding in her over the past few months, and I'd wanted to know more about where it was coming from. I asked her, "What do you long for now?"

"My longings are tender. I long to live free of fear of rejection, free of the fear of fear. I long to use this opportunity of exile to build compassion for those who have been exiled way longer than me—by the color of their skin or physical disability or whatever. I long to give to the world in a way that is a mix of my personality and experiences (this has been rekindled). Misappropriated power moves people to timidity; I long to right some of that."

I asked, "How much of that is a pipe dream or something that's actually possible?"

"Oh no, it's more than wishful thinking; it's possible. I can touch into my deepest core and stumble, in humility, and find this stuff."

My last question for Tessa was, "What is your longing for your daughter?"

She paused, thoughtful, and responded, "Months ago I would have said that I longed for her to never be in the situation I've been in. But as I'm finding this new place of hope, I'm realizing that I long for her to experience hope."

Tessa's small "hope basket" is still on the dresser in her room. She said, "It's still empty, but I think I'm close to putting things in it."

## A LIFETIME OF LONGING IN THE PRESENCE OF HOPE

I'd guess she was fourteen or fifteen when she found out she was pregnant. The fact that she was engaged didn't exactly make things better since her fiancé wasn't the father. Talk about a recipe for fear.

But when the angel explained things to Mary the mother of Jesus, she offered up one of the greatest statements of faith in the entire Bible: "I am the Lord's servant," Mary answered. "May your word to me be fulfilled" (Luke 1:38).

We see Mary as a paragon of Hope. The song she sang as an acknowledgment of what God was doing, the "Magnificat"—Latin for "(my soul) magnifies"—is one of the most hopeful passages in the Bible, especially considering her circumstances:

My soul glorifies the Lord
    and my spirit rejoices in God my Savior,

for he has been mindful
    of the humble state of his servant.

From now on all generations will call me blessed,
    for the Mighty One has done great things for me—
    holy is his name.

His mercy extends to those who fear him,
    from generation to generation.

He has performed mighty deeds with his arm;
    he has scattered those who are proud in their inmost thoughts.

He has brought down rulers from their thrones
    but has lifted up the humble.

He has filled the hungry with good things
    but has sent the rich away empty.

He has helped his servant Israel,
    remembering to be merciful

to Abraham and his descendants forever,
    just as he promised our ancestors. (Luke 1:46-55)

Can you imagine how Hope-full life must have been for Mary,

carrying the Hope-giver in her womb, then watching his life? Mary saw, before anyone else, the hints of Jesus' divinity shining through. At a human level, Mary would have had reason for Hope more than any other human who ever lived.

And yet, we *also* see in Mary a lifetime of longing. She lived "already, not yet" every minute of every day. Consider these scenes from Mary's life through this lens:

*Telling Joseph, her fiancé, about her pregnancy. Telling her family.*

*The birth of Jesus, in a smelly animal shed. Seeing Jesus worshiped by shepherds, but wondering what might come next.*

*Finding twelve-year-old Jesus missing after two days of travel, and returning to Jerusalem to find him engaged in robust dialogue with the temple priests.*

*Seeing Jesus turn water into wine at a wedding feast, in response to her request. But also hearing Jesus' caution not to tell anyone about the miracle.*

*Hearing Jesus teach, and knowing the revolutionary nature of his words. Seeing the crowds respond with adulation, and the religious leaders respond with scorn.*

*Watching or hearing about Jesus stirring the pot by eating with sinners, condemning the Pharisees, associating with those who were hated.*

*Hearing Jesus predict his own death.*

*Watching the people lay down a bed of palm branches for Jesus, on a donkey, to ride into town. Then seeing the people turn on him in a matter of hours, calling for his execution.*

*Seeing Jesus flogged and nailed on a cross for a humiliating and excruciating death, knowing that this was somehow still part of the plan.*

*Seeing the resurrected Jesus.*

Mary's life is, in many ways, the ultimate embodiment of the tango—Hope and longing inseparably intertwined. Mary, like us, might have been able to experience longing without Hope; but she couldn't experience real Hope without longing.

Four hundred years before he wrote them, Mary understood the words of Augustine: "The whole life of the good Christian is a holy longing. . . . That is our life, to be trained by longing."[5]

## TANGO IN RWANDA

You may be familiar with the story of Gary Haugen, founder of International Justice Mission. I had the good fortune of meeting Gary in the earliest days of IJM and sharing a significant spiritual moment for both of us. As a result, I've been encouraged by his friendship over the years, and by his wise council at various points in my own journey (including during my life crisis and exile I've written about in this book).

As a freshly minted lawyer, working for the United States Department of Justice, Gary was loaned to the United Nations to function as the Investigator in Charge following the 1994 Rwandan genocide.[6]

If you're not familiar with the Rwandan genocide, it was a very strange frenzied conflict between two (somewhat arbitrary and contrived) ethnic groups in Rwanda, the Hutu and the Tutsi. Aided and even coordinated by local and national government, military and mass media, Hutus slaughtered Tutsis and pro-peace Hutus. Over a relatively short period of one hundred days, eight hundred thousand people were killed (20 percent of the country's population), some at gunpoint but, as more civilians joined in the rampage and bullets grew scarce, often by machete.

Immediately following this slaughter, Gary landed in Rwanda to lead the UN investigation. Uncovering mass graves, churches heaped with bodies and death never more than steps away, Haugen wrestled with his easily earned (and therefore cheap) American notions of hope.

I asked Gary recently how he held on to Hope in those days. He said, "In a situation like that, there's an overwhelming of all the familiar handles you might have for finding hope—handholds you're used to grabbing on to in the boat of life. And then a tsunami hits, and those handles just aren't enough. That's what genocide is like. You see almost a million people butchered in a few weeks and it's overwhelming. You have to pass through that to get to the other side of what is real. The evil and slaughter and brutality is real and you have to face that if you ever want to see hope again."

Today, the International Justice Mission that Haugen started shortly after his work in Rwanda is composed of global leaders in bringing justice to the worst places of injustice—slavery, corruption, sex trade, illegal land grabs, unjust imprisonment and many other issues. IJM is a collection of more than "five hundred lawyers, investigators, social workers and other staff—approximately 95 percent of whom are nationals of the countries in which they serve."[7]

Having a courtside seat from which to watch IJM develop over the last fifteen years, I see them as an organizational embodiment of the idea we're talking about here. Millions of people around the world desire a world where justice is experienced, especially by those for whom it seems the most out of reach. But IJM's Hope—and Gary Haugen's Hope—is actively dancing with longing. And that longing is strongly captured in Isaiah 1:17: "Learn to do right; seek justice. Defend the oppressed. Take up the cause of the fatherless; plead the case of the widow." Those are marching orders for IJM because they long for a world—a world they are very hopeful about—where justice will be present and normal, within the reach of even the weakest and most marginalized.

That spinning motion of Hope and longing was, I believe, the momentum that got Gary Haugen through those horrendous months in Rwanda back in 1994, and it's the engine down in the belly of IJM's ship today.

Longing is gorgeous. Longing dreams of a new reality that Hope believes will be realized.

## TRANSFORMED LONGINGS

Our desires—our longings—have been with us since our time in exile. Our dissatisfactions are, in a sense, the opposite of our longings. Our honest and emotional cries out to God are an open-handed expression of those longings. But our longings don't disappear when Hope arrives. Instead, they're transformed in the tango with Hope.

Initially, our longing will primarily be self-centered. This is normal, and I'm not suggesting that people with longings about their own difficult circumstances are immature or particularly selfish (at least not any more than the rest of us). But over time, as Hope rushes in, those longings start to change.

The exiled Israelites in Egypt weren't exactly longing for the day they would embody God's promise to Abraham that they would be a blessing to the world (Genesis 12:2-3). They weren't even longing for a land flowing with milk and honey. That was so far off the radar that it never would have crossed their minds. Their longing—call it self-centered or selfish if you want—was a much more primal need, much more basic:

*I long to not experience the whip of my overseer today.*
*I long to make enough bricks that I won't get brutally punished.*
*I long to avoid being killed at the whim of someone who doesn't consider me human.*
*I long to survive.*

But once the Israelites entered the Promised Land (Hope's arrival, and the end of exile), they remembered God's words to Abraham. The focus of their longings shifted, and turned outward. Instead of a ceasing of the whip or escape from oppression, their longings shifted toward working the land, living in peace, worshiping God and setting up a just society.

Joshua, who replaced Moses and led the people into the Promised Land, said to them in Deuteronomy 26:19:

He has declared that he will set you in praise, fame and honor high above all the nations he has made and that you will be a people holy to the LORD your God, as he promised.

Once we pass through the semipermeable wall of fear and receive Hope, longing starts to morph, informed by and comingled with Hope.

Tessa (whose story I shared earlier in this chapter) was initially faced with extremely immediate longings: a place to live and food for her daughter. Now her longings are being transformed. Her desire for peace is a "next step" of sorts. And knowing Tessa and her giftedness, I'm quite confident that very soon she'll begin longing to use her abilities and creativity to have an impact on others.

If real Hope is *a faithful confidence that God continues to author a story that moves us from vision to action*, it's rare to discover the "action" part of that on day one of Hope's arrival. Instead, the arrival of Hope calms our anxious hearts and slowly, gently, lovingly, shifts our focus. Once our lives start to become post-exilic, the tango moves us across the dance floor of life, bringing an *expansiveness* and *generosity* to our longings (two traits that reflect the heart of God).

With transformed longings in the picture, we now have a complete image of the process I have come to see over and over again. It's the pattern in biblical stories and teaching. I've observed it (and you probably have also) in the lives of hopeful people around me. And I've seen it play out in my own life. Adding the tango of Hope and transformed longings to the diagram we've been building, we can finally complete it like this:

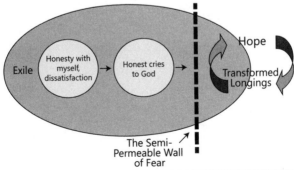

Figure 9.1

Can you find yourself in that process at this point in your life? Can you see, in hindsight, times you've moved through those stages?

# Hope Toolbox

- Take a few minutes (or more) to write down your deepest longings. Make the list as long as you can, and as fully worded as possible. Include longings about your own life, about your community and friends, and about the world in general. Prayerfully notice connections and themes, and notice which longings give you the most energy when you consider movement toward them.

- Reflect on the life of Mary, mother of Jesus. Pull out a Bible and read passages about her life in the Gospels. Consider the interplay of Hope and longing in her daily life, and how it does or doesn't align with your own experience.

- If your longings were to become *expansive* and *generous*, what might they look like? What specific *expansive* and *generous* longing gives you a sense of vision and excitement?

# TEN

# HOPECASTING

About a decade ago, I helped forge a partnership between the youth ministry organization where I worked and World Vision, the global aid and development organization. This came about as a result of hearing the statistic that, at the time, Christians were the least likely demographic group willing to donate two dollars to help an AIDS orphan. We found this nothing less than despicable, and set out to do something about it. We created One Life Revolution to help American youth groups learn about the AIDS pandemic in Africa and raise funds to make a difference, particularly for widows and orphans left behind.

As part of this initiative, World Vision took my coworker Tic Long and me to Zambia, to see firsthand the work these efforts would fund. World Vision Zambia had set up a schedule of visits that included communities at various points in the path of receiving help. And on our second day in the country, we met a group of brothers who had only come onto World Vision's radar in the past few days.

We drove on a paved two-lane road, about an hour outside of Lusaka. Then we drove another hour on a violently bumpy dirt road, stopping in what absolutely seemed like the middle of nowhere. It wasn't a village: there was simply one tiny dilapidated hut, about the size of a backyard storage shed, and barely standing. Knocking on the door, we were cautiously greeted by four brothers, ranging in age from fourteen down to five. In conversation, we learned that both of their parents had died of AIDS in the past year and they were completely on their own. They had an uncle who lived a few hundred yards away who looked in on them from time to time, but was not able to offer them much help. Really, it was astonishing that they were alive.

Of course, my heart was broken, and the faces of those boys framed the rest of my trip and stuck in my mind for years. Returning from the trip, I told the middle schoolers at my church about the brothers, the two oldest being the same age as kids in my youth group.

The hearts of these San Diego middle schoolers were moved; and in a beautiful way that keeps me working with kids this age, they wanted to *do something* about it. I'd mentioned in passing that $3,000 would provide these brothers, or others just like them, a new house. Combining passion and naiveté, a group of sixth through eighth graders decided at that moment that they were going to raise the funds.

Here's where I have to add my first confession pertaining to this story: I didn't think they could do it. I thought it was wonderful that they wanted to do something, and completely planned on supporting them in any way I could; but I thought it was more likely that they would raise a few hundred dollars than a few thousand dollars.

We considered multiple means of fundraising: bake sales, walk-athons, car washes. But somehow they got it in their heads that they wanted to put on a variety show. This would provide the opportunity to also tell stories of AIDS orphans combined with taking an offering. I was skeptical, but they were insistent.

They wanted to hold the variety show in the main church worship center, which seats something close to one thousand people. I pushed back that we should hold it in the middle school room, since I didn't think anyone other than their parents would attend. But they were insistent.

The evening of the One Night Revolution, hundreds of people showed up to support a couple dozen eleven- to fourteen-year-olds and whatever it was that they had been talking about with so much passion. Let's be clear: it was a variety show, not a talent show. A talent show, by definition, has talent. The titular distinction of this show was its variety. Case in point (I am *not* making this up): one act was a sixth-grade boy doing a hula-hoop routine to a disco song while wearing a silver sequined jumpsuit. Really.

Sprinkled throughout the show, we told stories about AIDS orphans in Zambia, and explained our goal of raising $3,000 to build a house. When the offering was counted, we'd collected $25,000. I've rarely felt so stunned (that's the best word for it) by the movement of God. Our senior pastor came up on stage, almost crying, and talked about how our middle schoolers had brought their lunches of loaves and fishes, and how Jesus had multiplied their gifts.

The middle schoolers, however, were not all that stunned. They weren't cocky, but they weren't shocked because they had *way* more faith than I did. I asked them what we should do with that much money. We could fund multiple houses. Or I'd seen how a clean water well could transform a community, and we had enough money to fund two wells. The kids prayed and voted to fund the wells.

A year later, the middle schoolers wanted to do it all again. And, once again, I was skeptical. I don't think I actually said these words out loud (I hope I didn't), but my faithless, Hope-less thinking was, "We got *lucky* last year." I remember some faith-filled, hopeful kid saying to me, "It doesn't matter if we raise $25,000 again or not. It only matters that we do our part."

Sigh. Out of the mouths of babes, and all that.

The second year, $35,000 was donated, and after prayer, the group of young teens voted to fund a medical clinic for the same community who had received clean water wells.

Today, a community of real people in Zambia has been dramatically changed. I'm sure things aren't perfect there, but restoration is in process. Hope arrived, and the longings of the people in that community started being transformed. And a group of now young adults in San Diego, who will likely never visit Zambia or meet the people in that village, received a double portion of Hope when their longings turned toward joining up with the present kingdom work of Jesus.

## THE BEST LIFE

The age-old existential question that has haunted philosophers and college sophomores for a very long time is some version of *Why am I here?* Jesus gives us some fodder for consideration in what has become my favorite Bible verse:

> I have come that they may have life, and have it to the full. (John 10:10)

Remember: When Jesus says "they" in this verse, he's talking about you.

Contrary to what one might assume by observing Christians in America, Jesus did *not* say:

> *I have come that you may get into heaven.*
> *I have come that you may leave this lousy place one day in the future.*
> *I have come that you may get serious about religion, finally.*
> *I have come that you may experience your ship coming in.*
> *I have come that you may know who's "in" and who's "out."*
> *I have come that you may stop disgusting me so much.*

It's a pretty revolutionary promise, really. Jesus wants you to experience a full life. That's his verbatim explanation for why he came to earth.

Why are you here? To have a full life. So, what's a full life, then?

I'm convinced from Scripture, observation of hopeful people and my own experience that a fullness of life burns most hot when I follow in the footsteps of Jesus and give my life away, bringing Hope to the hopeless. This, my friends, is Hopecasting.

As my more self-focused longings are filled with the pigment of Hope, they start to shift. Since Hope and longing are dancing the tango, a shift in one shifts the other. My Hope increases, and my longings turn outward. My longings grow more expansive and my Hope needs a power boost. As that symbiotic swirl becomes more unrestrained, open and generous, the Hope in us—"the glorious riches of this mystery, which is Christ in you, the hope of glory" (Colossians 1:27)—casts off onto those around us. Indeed, we begin Hopecasting to the whole world.

This is the full life. This is the life we were invented for. This is God's dream for you, a continual broadening of your longings and increase of Hope put into action.

## GOD IS THE BIGGER ELVIS

In the 1960s, Dolores Hart was a Hollywood movie starlet with an extremely bright future. After she starred opposite Elvis Presley in the 1957 film *Loving You*, the Hollywood press considered her the next big thing. Ten films followed in five years, working with big male leads such as Montgomery Clift, Robert Wagner and George Hamilton.

But Dolores walked away from everything amidst a crisis of faith, and became a cloistered nun at the Abbey of Regina Laudis in Connecticut. Cloistered nuns are those who, in addition to the vows other nuns take, live in a nunnery that is walled off. They never leave (other than for a medical emergency), though an important aspect of their ministry is usually meeting with people who come to them. Dolores says, "I never felt I was leaving Hollywood. I never felt I was leaving anything that I was given. The abbey was like a grace of God that just entered my life in a way that was totally unexpected. And God was the vehicle. He was the bigger Elvis."

Dolores is still alive today. Her beautiful and touching story is told in a wonderful documentary, *God Is the Bigger Elvis*, which can be viewed in its entirety on YouTube.[1] Feel free to go watch it. I'll wait here.

On the surface, the life of a cloistered nun would seem the exact opposite of the full life Jesus invites us into, a life of joining up with his work in the word, bringing Hope to the hopeless. But watching the documentary, it becomes clear that Hopecasting is Dolores Hart's vocation. Living almost obsessively, relentlessly postured for the presence of Jesus, Dolores has plenty of Hope to cast. Near the end of the film, she says, "People come to speak to us about every possible form of suffering that hits the human heart. My role is to help the person to discover that you can always find hope; and if you can find hope, you might find faith."

## NEED BECOMES HOPE BECOMES ACTION
## BECOMES HOPECASTING

Bartimaeus had his pathetic act down to a science. As a man blind from birth, he'd had few to no other options in life. His extended family, assuming he had them, needed him to help financially in *some* way. So begging was his job description.

There were rules and protocols to this sort of thing, of course. Bartimaeus knew the *appropriate* words to use and the best volume. He knew how often to repeat his pleas. He knew the best place to sit, and the most productive body language and facial expression. He'd been doing it all his life and had perfected the art as much as anyone could.

This craft was about one thing and one thing only: money.

Bart wasn't out there begging for sight. That, of course, would have been absurd.

But then, along comes Jesus (read the whole story in Mark 10:46-52). Imagine the scene: Jesus is walking down the road where Bartimaeus sits, out of the way, avoiding tripping feet or crossing the subtle line into annoyance (which he'd found decreased donations). Jesus isn't alone, of course. He's got his posse with him, and dozens of other hangers-on, shuffling along like they have bungee cords between them and this Rabbi. They've attached themselves, in this moment, for a wide variety of reasons: *I want to hear this guy; I'm hoping he'll do a*

*magic trick; There's something compelling about this man; I hope to catch
him teaching heresy; This man might be a threat to my power.*

Bartimaeus hears the amoeba-like crowd passing by, catches a few
audible snippets, connects the dots with rumors he's heard and decides
to break convention.

Bartimaeus starts shouting out, "Jesus, Son of David, have mercy
on me!"

Social contract about appropriate volumes for begging: broken.

Social contract about the number of times a beggar can ask for
help: broken.

Social contract about not bothering important visiting dignitaries:
broken.

It's clear that Bartimaeus is being annoying and inappropriate because "many" rebuked him and told him to shut up. But good ol' Bart,
he was just beginning to put the dissatisfaction of his exile into an
honest cry to God.

Amidst the shushing and "Pipe down, man!" and "Know your
place!" comments, Bartimaeus shouted *louder* and *repeatedly*. (Note:
there's nothing wrong with repeating your honest cries to God over
and over again.)

Jesus stops and simply says, "Call him."

There are a few mildly humorous bits in this story, and what
happens next is one of them. The shushers and rebukers instantly
change their tune. You can almost hear their thoughts, "Oh, Jesus
wants to talk to him. Okay, well, I don't want to be seen in opposition
to that, so let me quickly position myself as an intermediary."

They say, "Cheer up! On your feet! He's calling you." (Read: Slap a
smile on your face! Be optimistic!)

Bartimaeus's response is anything but passive or lazy or wary or
skeptical. He throws off his robe and jumps to his feet.

Jesus asks an interesting question: "What do you want me to do
for you?"

I love that question. The *obvious* answer to everyone who'd ever seen Bartimaeus or his kind on the side of the road was "I want money." But Jesus is pushing in, giving Bart a chance to verbalize his deeper longing. In a way, Jesus is asking, "Are you aware that Hope is just now visiting you? Are you willing to step into that Hope? Or would you prefer to stay in exile?"

Bartimaeus blurts out an absurd statement, a deep longing, that he's surely never before verbalized to someone along the road. In fact, he'd long ago given up on the idea that things might change. Bart, almost breathlessly, exhales the words, "Rabbi, I want to see."

Jesus, of course, responds that Bart's faith has healed him (a fascinating phrase that deserves exploration elsewhere), and Bart's vision is immediately restored. He's been blind since birth, so the very first thing Bartimaeus sees with his newly minted sight is the face of Jesus.

There's plenty of awesome stuff in this story. But the very last phrase is the one that challenges me, particularly since Jesus' words to Bartimaeus are "Go, your faith has healed you."

Immediately he received his sight and followed Jesus along the road. (Mark 10:52)

I have to ask myself, what would I have done if I were Bartimaeus? I imagine myself blind since birth, having spent a lifetime begging on the side of a road, longing for sight but assuming it was a silly pipe-dream. Then, suddenly, in a matter of seconds, I'd been granted sight. What's the first thing I would do? And the second thing? And how would I spend that first day, and week, and month?

Honestly, I'm just not convinced I would follow Jesus down the road. Maybe I would, though. Maybe the only reasonable response to longings being met is to follow the trail of the Hope that brought you to satisfaction in the first place.

Following Jesus. That reminds me of something IJM's Gary Haugen said to me during our chat about Hope: "I find ultimate hope in the midst of justice work here on earth, because God is still in the business of transforming his kingdom here on earth, and his way—goodness, justice, love—will ultimately rule. God is doing that work, and we get into the wake of his work in the world—we follow him."

## THE LEAGUE OF HOPECASTERS IS ACCEPTING MEMBERS

Following Jesus is a response to Hope, and it propels the tango of Hope and revitalized, revolutionized longings. Some longings stay with us but get reframed, others simply fall by the wayside, and still more—the partnering with Jesus sort—get birthed, and spray out like a lawn sprinkler:

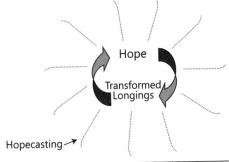

**Figure 10.1**

The Hopecasting life is *not* waiting around for a heavenly afterlife. The Hopecasting life is an active life of carrying Hope as you interact with the world.

I've previously mentioned my friend Jon Huckins, whose peace-making work in the Middle East (and in his own urban neighborhood in San Diego) is a continual challenge and encouragement to me. Jon gave me some great insights into the posture of being a Hopecaster.

When he first started his work, his natural assumption was that his role was to engage in politics. But Palestinians and Israelis wisely told Jon, "Do not come here and take our conflict home with you. Come and hear our stories—Jew, Muslim and Christian throughout Israel and Palestine—and share the stories back at home in a way that honors the inhabitants of the land, so we can engage people on a human level rather than a political level."

Jon shared with me his thinking about where the Western church has failed in peacemaking, and it's all about the shape of our Hope: "In the West, we only hear stories through media channels that are funded by telling stories of violence, division and brokenness. We (especially Christians) lose our prophetic imagination about what could be—we have a *fatalistic* theology—believing this will only be fixed when Jesus returns. This is sin, because we do harm to our brothers and sisters (of any faith) living in Israel and the West Bank. Jesus came to bring a *hopeful* theology—the Kingdom is here, and the restoration has already begun. We're agents of that. As soon as hope is taken out of the equation, we fail to be true to our faith.

"Isn't it Christian hope that should move us toward conflict? I've found the most advanced hope bearers anywhere in the world are in the Middle East. Living as someone with hope is gritty, subversive and countercultural. At a macro level it can feel as if there is no hope. Where we find hope is in the reality we create every day with our actions as we choose to live, love and lead in the ways of Jesus."

Jon quoted Milad, a Christian man working in a hotel with tourists but running a ministry in Bethany working with 99 percent Muslim children: "Hope for us is knowing that we're following the Prince of Peace in the experiences of the greatest hostility and suffering possible. And when we do that faithfully, we see the impossible unfold."

Jon summarized: "As Christians, the places where hope seems impossible are exactly the places we're supposed to inhabit, because we trust the end of the story. When we don't do that, we continue to feed stories of brokenness and division and give in to lives of hopelessness."

There it is: a faithful confidence that God continues to author a story that moves us from vision to action. In action, and for others, Hope becomes Hopecasting.

Theologian Jürgen Moltmann writes, "Hope alone is to be called 'realistic,' because it alone takes seriously the possibilities with which all reality is fraught. It does not take things as they happen to stand or to lie, but as a progressing, moving thing with possibilities of change."[2]

Brueggemann puts it this way: "What is the function of hope? Why is hope practiced? What happens when a people hopes? The answer I make is: hope keeps the present arrangement open and pro-visional. Hope reminds us that the way things are (and all the ex-trapolations we make from that), is precarious and in jeopardy. Hope reminds us not to absolutize the present, not to take it too seriously, not to treat it too honorably, because it will not last."[3]

If this rallying cry to an active life of Hope all sounds overwhelming in your current place of exile, soak for a bit in the words of Isaiah:

Do you not know?
> Have you not heard?

The LORD is the everlasting God,
> the Creator of the ends of the earth.

He will not grow tired or weary,
> and his understanding no one can fathom.

He gives strength to the weary
> and increases the power of the weak. (Isaiah 40:28-29)

## THE END OF HOPE

Hopecasting is the very best life, the dream of God for you. But there's something *even better* than a life of Hopecasting. And that's what comes *next*.

Hope will one day become completely unnecessary for those who, like Bartimaeus, follow Jesus. The tango will stop, not because the party's over, but because the party is starting. Longings will forever and completely be met.

I've sometimes helped teenagers think about the big-picture story of the Bible by using "episode" titles I found years ago (and slightly modified) in the book *The Story We Find Ourselves In*.[4] Those seven episodes are:

*Creation:* God's loving and perfect dream becoming reality

*Crisis:* sin and brokenness entering the story

*Call:* Abraham's selection to be blessed and be a blessing

*Conversation:* God's interaction with God's people, focused on righteousness

*Christ:* God coming to us, bringing the kingdom of heaven to earth

*Community:* the development of the church, the body of Christ, charged with being Hopecasters

And the seventh chapter: *Commencement.*[5] Commencement is a wonderful idea. Consider a high school graduation. It's a ceremony—a point in time—that marks a significant transition point. Commencement, as a word, refers to starting or launching. But as a ceremony, it's both *the end of something* and *the start of something new.*

Commencement is what's ahead for us—that time and place when Jesus completes his promised restoration of everything. Commencement is the culmination of Jesus' redemption and ultimate salvation. Commencement is the end of longings since in complete perfection there will be nothing to long for. And with the cessation of longings, the purpose of Hope also ceases to be necessary or relevant.

Paul writes:

> We ourselves, who have the firstfruits of the Spirit, groan inwardly as we wait eagerly for our adoption to sonship, the redemption of our bodies. For in this hope we were saved. But hope that is seen is no hope at all. Who hopes for what they already have? But if we hope for what we do not yet have, we wait for it patiently. (Romans 8:23-25)

At commencement, when all is restored, our deepest longings and our Hope will be perfectly and fully met—satisfied, in the deepest sense of that word.

But commencement is also the launch of something new. The "already but not yet" kingdom gives way to the "already and eternal." When this happens, the words from the Lord's Prayer—"*your kingdom come, your will be done, on earth as it is in heaven*" (Matthew 6:10)—become past tense. Instead, post-commencement earth is synonymous with heaven. We will have followed Jesus through resurrection and into immortality. We'll no longer need a mediator, as we'll be in the unmediated presence of God.

For now, we live as Hopecasters, by faith, on earth as it is in heaven. But one day we will be vindicated in that Hope, and our faith will be rewarded with sight.

Slowly read these words, from Hebrews 10:32-39, remembering the journey toward Hopecasting, and the hopeful journey toward the commencement of our future, immortal lives in the perfect kingdom of God:

> Remember those earlier days after you had received the light, when you endured in a great conflict full of suffering. Sometimes you were publicly exposed to insult and persecution; at other times you stood side by side with those who were so treated. You suffered along with those in prison and joyfully accepted the confiscation of your property, because you knew that you yourselves had better and lasting possessions. So do not throw away your confidence; it will be richly rewarded.
>
> You need to persevere so that when you have done the will of God, you will receive what he has promised. For,

> "In just a little while,
>     he who is coming will come
>     and will not delay."

And,

"But my righteous one will live by faith.
    And I take no pleasure
    in the one who shrinks back."

But we do not belong to those who shrink back and are destroyed,
but to those who have faith and are saved.

## Hope Toolbox

- If Jesus came to give you a full life, what do you imagine that would look like (try to separate yourself from any material or immediate desires, and consider a full life that is *expansive* and generous)? If your longings turn outward, what vision and ideas come to mind?

- Reflect on the story of Bartimaeus receiving his sight, putting yourself in his sandals. What would you have done in the first hour after receiving your sight? Here's a challenging question for consideration: What does following Jesus look like?

- We're invited to live an "active life of carrying Hope as you interact with the world." What might that look like for you in the next twelve months? What are the implications of keeping "the present arrangement open and provisional"?

# ACKNOWLEDGMENTS

This book either would not exist, or would have been significantly weaker, were it not for:

The four people who read the first draft and gave me helpful reproof, correction, encouragement and suggestions: Jeannie Oestreicher, Rod Dunlap, Sam Saavedra and Morgan Schmidt.

The two theologians who were gentle, wise and insightful in their feedback on the first draft: Ed Noble and Blair Bertrand. I'm so glad you didn't burn it to the ground and call me a heretic. Your comments and suggestions have, hopefully, saved me from looking like an idiot in more than a few places.

Butch and Ann Whitely, whose desert home in Canebrake Canyon was not only the place where much of this book was written, but was also the location of some liminal moments in my journey that shaped my experience of and thinking about Hope.

The friends who allowed me to interview them and share parts of their stories in this book: Sam Saavedra, Alex Roller, Tessa, Gary Haugen and Jon Huckins. Your vulnerability, honesty and insight were the reasons I was confident in asking for your help.

My literary agent and friend, Greg Daniel, who believed in this book even after more than one publisher said "I don't get it" and "a book about hope won't sell."

Dave Zimmerman from IVP for championing this book and pushing me harder than I've ever been pushed by an editor. I was thrilled when IVP agreed to publish this book because I knew Dave was the perfect combination of brilliant and brutally tough. If this book has clarity, it's due to Dave's insight and guidance. Thanks also to the rest of the team at IVP for welcoming my book to your stable of always high-quality works.

Countless friends, particularly youth workers, who in face-to-face conversations and Facebook comments encouraged my writing along the way.

Adam McLane, my partner in The Youth Cartel, for never once hinting that I was taking too much time away from our work in order to write, and for voicing his excitement for me in this "step of faith."

My church—Journey Community Church—for being a consistently Hope-filled community, a place overflowing with people whose lives have been revolutionized by Hope.

My family—Jeannie, Riley and Max—who were gracious and understanding about my apparent inability to write at home and my need to get away, and patient when I talked about my progress too much.

## A WORD OF ACKNOWLEDGMENT AND ATTRIBUTION TO WALTER BRUEGGEMANN

When this book was proposed and acquired by IVP Books, I didn't actually realize I was going to be writing something of a popular-level book of theology. Really, it was only as I got into the writing process, often feeling very out of my league, that I realized I was suggesting a framework that needed to be more than my puny opinions. Walter Brueggemann was my guide.

Walter Brueggemann is a retired minister, author, theologian (does anyone actually *retire* from theology?) and professor. He is widely considered one of the most important Old Testament theologians of the last several decades.

In some ways, this book might have been called *Brueggemann for Dummies* (though Brueggemann might very well distance himself from that affiliation). And while I certainly quote from him and attribute him many times throughout this book, my proposals and ruminations were informed by his work in ways that go beyond those citations.

I was aware of Brueggemann but hadn't read any of his books when I first started toying with the idea of writing a book about Hope more than four years ago. I'd been asked to speak on Hope at a denominational retreat for youth workers and felt I should do a bit of reading in preparation. While on a silent retreat in the same desert location where I wrote most of this book, I devoured Brueggemann's *Hope Within History* (I had two of his other books with me, but didn't read them until much later), scribbling in the margins and high-lighting passages on every other page. I felt like I'd found a conversation partner—a mentor—to help me better frame the impulses and intuitive notions I was forming about Hope. And while I would certainly say that my early thoughts were biblically informed in general, Brueggemann's work provided a confidence that I wasn't crazy or exegetically misguided.

So much of what has been written about Hope focuses almost exclusively on heaven. The emphasis of that message was troubling to me, and provided neither the best understanding of the Bible's teaching on Hope nor the daily fuel I want and need for a full, passionate life. But Brueggemann's books were different, going old school with Old Testament anchoring in the stories of the Exodus and the Prophets (particularly Isaiah).

There *may* be places in this book where an astute theologian would wonder if I was plagiarizing Brueggemann. While I can say that I've tried to be very careful not to steal thoughts without attribution, let this be an acknowledgment that every other page in this book could probably have a Brueggemann footnote on it, and I hope this page covers my absolute appreciation and indebtedness.

# FURTHER READING

Brueggemann, Walter. *Hope Within History*. Atlanta, GA: John Knox Press, 1987.

———. *Hopeful Imagination: Prophetic Voices in Exile*. Minneapolis: Fortress, 1986.

———. *The Prophetic Imagination*. Minneapolis: Fortress, 1978.

Haugen, Gary. *Good News About Injustice: A Witness of Courage in a Hurting World*. Downers Grove, IL: InterVarsity Press, 2009.

Jones, Tony. *A Better Atonement: Beyond the Depraved Doctrine of Original Sin*. Minneapolis: The JoPa Group, 2012.

McKnight, Scot. *A Community Called Atonement: Living Theology*. Nashville: Abingdon, 2007.

Moltmann, Jürgen. *Theology of Hope*. Translated by James W. Leitch. Minneapolis: Fortress, 1993.

Nouwen, Henri J. M. *With Open Hands*. Notre Dame, IN: Ave Maria Press, 2006.

Wright, N. T. *Surprised by Hope: Rethinking Heaven, the Resurrection, and the Mission of the Church*. San Francisco: HarperOne, 2008.

# NOTES

### 1. I WANT HOPE

[1]*Merriam-Webster Dictionary*, www.merriam-webster.com/dictionary/hope, "hope."

[2]Dave Eggers, *The Circle* (San Francisco: McSweeney's Books, 2013), p. 332.

[3]Bryan Loritts, presentation at The Youth Cartel event, The Summit, Marietta, GA, November 9, 2013.

[4]Big thanks to Blair Bertrand for helping me wrangle the wording on this definition.

### 2. EXILE: LIFE WITHOUT HOPE

[1]Quoted in Steven Naifeh and Gregory White Smith, *Van Gogh: The Life* (New York: Random House, 2011), p. 124.

[2]See Ichak Adizes, *Pursuit of Prime* (Santa Barbara, CA: Adizes Institute, 2005).

### 3. IDENTIFYING HOPE'S ENEMIES

[1]Walter Brueggemann's descriptions of hope's enemies are profound and helpful. I've adapted three of them here (Hope Enemies 3-5), but you can find his take on them in chapter 4 of *Hope Within History* (Atlanta, GA: John Knox Press, 1987).

[2]Brueggemann, *Hope Within History*, p. 89.

### 4. POSITIONING FOR HOPE: HONESTY WITH OURSELVES

[1]Walter Brueggemann, *Hope Within History* (Atlanta, GA: John Knox Press, 1987), p. 32.

[2]Ibid., pp. 38, 47.

### 5. POSITIONING FOR HOPE: HONEST CRIES TO GOD

[1]I don't believe it's anthropomorphic—ascribing human characteristics to God—to claim that God has emotions. There are simply too many biblical

references to dismiss the idea of God having emotion, not the least of which is that we—and our emotions—are created in the image of God. But this is not to say that our emotions are exactly the same as God's experience of emotions. We are created in the image of God, but we are not god(s).

[2]We should acknowledge that we don't really know exactly when Jesus "got" a body. We know some about his human body after his birth on earth, and get hints about his transfigured body after the resurrection; but we really don't know if he had "form" or "body" prior to his birth in Bethlehem. Theologians debate this point because it shapes the implications of the fact that we are made in the image of God.

[3]G. Walter Hansen, "The Emotions of Jesus," *Christianity Today*, February 3, 1997, www.christianitytoday.com/ct/1997/february3/7t2042.html.

[4]As I've noted elsewhere, I want to be careful not to project all our human traits on any of the three persons of the Trinity (called anthropomorphism). But there isn't a compelling reason to believe, from what we see in Scripture, that the Holy Spirit doesn't experience some version of emotion, even if we concede that when we consider this "we see only a reflection as in a mirror" (1 Corinthians 13:12).

[5]Henri J. M. Nouwen, *With Open Hands*, (Notre Dame, IN: Ave Maria Press, 2006).

[6]One of the theologians who reviewed this manuscript for me, Blair Bertrand, provided some helpful input on this idea: "Karl Barth would call this correspondence. God's grace is openhanded towards us and elicits a response of openhanded gratitude. A kiss calls for a kiss, a handshake, a handshake, and so God's action towards us calls for an action in response. We cannot act unless God acts, but we can act." We act *because* God acts!

## 6. THE PUSHBACK: FEAR

[1]The darkest version of this fear, by the way, is "Maybe God doesn't exist."

[2]Renee Altson, *Stumbling Toward Faith* (Grand Rapids: Zondervan, 2004). This excellent book is out of print; but it's available on Kindle and the author is giving away the remaining stock for free to anyone who emails her: renee.a@gmail.com.

[3]Walter Brueggemann, *Hope Within History* (Atlanta, GA: John Knox Press, 1987), p. 41.

[4]To learn more about Daoud and his organization, go to www.tentofnations.org.

## 7. JESUS, THE HOPE-BRINGER

[1]I find it worthy of a snicker that Doctor Luke didn't include that bit about his professional peers.

[2]I was first introduced to this fact by Sara Miles in *Jesus Freak* (San Francisco: Jossey-Bass, 2010).

[3]While I heard Yaconelli tell this story in talks, he wrote about it in his excellent book *Dangerous Wonder* (Colorado Springs: NavPress, 2003).

[4]N. T. Wright, *Surprised by Hope: Rethinking Heaven, the Resurrection, and the Mission of the Church* (San Francisco: HarperOne, 2008).

[5]My thinking in this section was greatly helped by Scot McKnight, *A Community Called Atonement* (Nashville: Abingdon, 2007); Tony Jones, *A Better Atonement* (Minneapolis: The JoPa Group, 2012); and N. T. Wright, *Surprised by Hope*.

## 8. HOPE'S ARRIVAL

[1]Matthew Henry, *Matthew Henry's Concise Commentary on the Bible*, Luke 19, www.biblegateway.com/resources/commentaries/Matthew-Henry/Luke/Conversion-Zaccheus.

[2]As I wrote in a note for chapter 5, some theologians might be uncomfortable (not in disagreement—just uncomfortable) with my language of partnering. Karl Barth calls this interaction "correspondence," with the idea that all of our actions, including what some would call obedience, are in response to God's actions on our behalf. I completely agree with that framing, but find the language of partnership to be more helpful in our current cultural context.

[3]Jürgen Moltmann, *Theology of Hope*, trans. James W. Leitch (Minneapolis: Fortress, 1993), p. 25.

[4]Walter Brueggemann, *Hope Within History* (Atlanta, GA: John Knox Press, 1987), p. 43.

## 9. HOPE'S DANCE PARTNER: TRANSFORMED LONGINGS

[1]Description of "Tango," Imperial Dance Studio, Gainesville, FL, www.imperial dancestudio.net/tango.html.

[2]*Encyclopaedia Brittanica*, www.britannica.com/EBchecked/topic/271447/hope, "hope."

[3]*Merriam-Webster Thesaurus*, www.merriam-webster.com/thesaurus/hope, "hope."

[4]*Wikipedia*, http://en.wikipedia.org/wiki/Kingdom_theology, "Kingdom theology."

[5]Augustine, *Later Works* (Louisville, KY: Westminster John Knox Press, 2008), p. 290.

[6]Read the full story in Gary's excellent book, *Good News About Injustice* (Downers Grove, IL: InterVarsity Press, 2009).

[7]To learn more about International Justice Mission, go to their website at www.ijm.org.

## 10. HOPECASTING

[1]*God Is the Bigger Elvis*, HBO Documentary Films, 2012, www.youtube /C8kvbkxmoHg.

[2]Jürgen Moltmann, *Theology of Hope*, trans. James W. Leitch (Minneapolis: Fortress, 1993), p. 25.

[3]Walter Brueggemann, *Hope Within History* (Atlanta, GA: John Knox Press, 1987), p. 80.

[4]Brian D. McLaren, *The Story We Find Ourselves In* (San Francisco: Jossey-Bass, 2008).

[5]In *The Story We Find Ourselves In*, McLaren uses the word *consummation*, but I haven't found that word to be all that helpful when talking to teenagers!

# THE YOUTH CARTEL

The Youth Cartel's mission is to encourage and challenge adults who minister to youth through holistic professional coaching, strategic consulting, transformational events, and inventive resource development that advance youth ministry in new ways.

**Save 20% off your next order with coupon code: nc15hc**

Visit our online store at theyouthcartel.com